GENESIS

Awakening From The Dream

GENESIS

Awakening From The Dream

Virginia Stephenson

I-Level
Acropolis Books, Publisher

Lakewood, CO　　　　　　Austell, GA

GENESIS
Awakening from the Dream
© 1987, 1997 Virginia Stephenson
All rights reserved
First edition 1987
New and expanded edition 1997

Edited by Carolyn and Bill Bauer

Unless otherwise specified, all Bible quotations
are taken from THE KING JAMES VERSION

Published by Acropolis Books, under its *I*-Level imprint

Printed in the United States of America.

Acropolis Books, Inc.
Lakewood, Colorado

http://www.acropolisbooks.com
————••✂••————
Cover design by
Studio 2 Graphic Arts, Ltd.
Denver, Colorado

LIBRARY OF CONGRESS CATALOGING-IN-PUBLICATION DATA

Stephenson, Virginia.
    Genesis: awakening from the dream / Virginia Stephenson. - - New
and expanded ed.
        p. cm.
    Includes bibliographical references.
    ISBN 1-889051-18-7 (pbk. : alk. paper)
    1. Bible. O. T. Genesis I-III--Spiritualistic interpretations.
    2. Creation--Miscellanea. 3. Eden--Mysticism. 4. Fall of man-
- Miscellanea. 5. Mysticism.   I. Title.
BS 1235.5.S68   1997
222' .11068- dc21   97–11242
                                                                CIP

THIS BOOK IS PRINTED ON ACID FREE PAPER THAT MEETS STANDARD
Z 39.48 OF THE AMERICAN NATIONAL STANDARDS INSTITUTE

Table of Contents

Table of Contents

Author's Note

Consciousness is forever unfolding at the level of realization. The two creation allegories presented in the first, second, and third chapters of Genesis reveal very different levels of consciousness, which result in very different conclusions about God, man, and the universe.

The original compilers of the Bible put first the allegory that expresses the spiritual principle of Oneness and the perfection of Being, and second, the story of Adam and Eve, who were expelled from the Garden of Eden. We begin our study with this story in Genesis 2 and 3, because when this allegory is clearly understood, those who ask, "Why do bad things happen to good people?" will find their answer and then be more receptive to the principle of creation as revealed in Genesis 1.

My teaching has always focused on the spiritual principles of the Bible, and over the years my lectures have emphasized the principles revealed in these two allegories. With the loving assistance of Carolyn and Bill Bauer, many hours of class-work were distilled into this book. For their editorial help with the original version and this revised edition, I am eternally grateful.

Joel Goldsmith, my teacher, always said to me, "Catch the idea, Virginia." This study of the two

Author's Note

versions of creation in Genesis will enable you to catch the idea of mystical Oneness, which is beyond words and thoughts, and thus awaken from the Adam dream.

Part I
Promise

The Inward Journey

The inward journey is not a journey in time and space but a change of direction inward to discover the spiritual capacities that each of us embodies. Few people have experienced the dynamics, the power, and the depth of their spiritual nature, but the fact that you have opened this book is an indication that you have been touched by the Spirit and that you are journeying inward.

A journey without a road map can be haphazard and difficult, whereas with guidance and direction we reach our destination more easily. The allegories and symbols of the Bible serve as helpful guides, directing us on our inward journey. Although spiritual teachers of long ago understood the spiritual significance of these stories and symbols, over the centuries much of the inner meaning of the Bible has been hidden or misinterpreted.

According to St. Jerome, "The most difficult and most obscure of the sacred books, Genesis, contains as many secrets as words, and each word contains several others." Seekers of truth have struggled to understand why there are two stories of creation in this first book of the Bible. They try to reconcile the two, but this cannot be done. The two versions of creation have remained side by side for centuries, one, a revelation telling mankind the nature of spiritual consciousness, the other, an analysis of the nature of human consciousness. Mystics have contemplated these two stories and have discovered secrets about the spiritual relationship of Oneness and about the working of the mind.

Yet even though these allegories are clearly understood by those of spiritual sense, they remain a mystery to those uninitiated into the truth of Being. Although we use our intellectual faculties to interpret human experiences, it is our spiritual faculties that reveal hidden meanings pertaining to spiritual experiences. Scripture must be interpreted with our spiritual sense, not with our intellect.

The purpose of this study of the Genesis versions of creation is to expand our awareness of the kingdom of God within us so that we can catch the spiritual sense of prayer. What we believe to be true about creation determines our understanding of the nature of God and the nature of prayer. If we understand the first chapter of Genesis, we have a God of Spirit, Light, and Love and a spiritual mode of prayer. If we accept the version of creation in the second and third chapters of Genesis, we have a God who rewards and punishes, who gives and withholds, and a totally different kind of prayer. The fundamental level of our state of awareness depends upon what concepts we accept to be true about creation.

The language of Spirit is a new tongue. Such common words as *day* or *night* have deep spiritual significance. Let us not consider *day* and *night* as opposites, but as the one Consciousness disclosing Itself in degrees. *Day* can mean a solar day, but it can also mean a period of inspiration and illumination. It is in this latter context that *day* is used in Genesis 1.

Night must not be thought of as an evil or negative experience, but rather as a period in which we wait for the undisclosed, or the hidden, to be revealed. The Psalmist said, ". . . the darkness hideth not from thee; but the night shineth as the day: the darkness and the light are both alike to thee."[1] Here the Psalmist realizes that nothing real and true can be hidden from our spiritual sense, which knows the truth. "Unto the upright there ariseth light in the darkness . . . ."[2] So it is with us. As we study and meditate upon Scripture, the light dawns in our awareness and reveals all that is hidden so that we can say, "I see; I understand."

Numbers also have hidden significance that helps us understand the meaning of Hebrew literature. The number *seven* signifies completeness. In the unfolding story of creation, the seven days of spiritual creation correspond to our sevenfold spiritual experience. "Six days thou shalt do thy work, and on the seventh day thou shalt rest."[3] Our six days are periods of discovery and revelation; the seventh day is our Sabbath, when we rest in the realization of omnipresent grace and fulfillment. Therefore, the seven days signify the completed spiritual idea and not that creation was finished in

eternity

seven solar days. Time is no part of spiritual creation, because time and space are material concepts. Through spiritual discernment we accept the principle that past, present, and future are united in the eternal Now.

λ   Genesis 1 presents a mystical view of creation, an individual unfoldment of the kingdom of God within us. It discloses the divine nature and character of God and our relationship of Oneness with this Source. Spirit, alone, is the activity, cause, and substance of all that is disclosed in Genesis 1.

Jesus, our great exemplar, said, "Think not that I am come to destroy the law, or the prophets: I am not come to destroy, but to fulfill."[4] The one infinite Consciousness includes the law and the prophetic nature, both of which are fulfilled by grace and truth. One can be obedient to the law consciousness but not have the prophetic consciousness, because to hear the word of Truth requires mystical awareness.

We see in Moses' experience how he was led by mystical awareness to the revelation of God's name when "he turned aside to see the burning bush that was not consumed."[5] God revealed to him His Name, "I AM THAT I AM" [Existence aware of Itself].[6] In his mountaintop experience, Moses was given the Ten Commandments, the law for individual self-government. These laws are a significant road map for harmonizing society.

Elijah, the great prophet, was taught by God in his mountaintop experience that power is not in material forces. God revealed that spiritual power is not in wind, earthquakes, or fire, but in "the still, small voice."[7] *Prophet* means one who hears and voices God's word.

A study of the Book of Isaiah indicates that there were two prophets called *Isaiah*. The one whose writings begin with Chapter 40 used *Isaiah* as his pen name, and no one knows who this Second Isaiah was. He has been credited with imparting to us the first chapter of Genesis, and he has been called The First Coming of the Messiah. I have quoted freely from both Isaiahs, because there are so many wonderful passages that highlight the text and demonstrate the mystical truth that was realized by these great prophets of the Old Testament.

Since most of us have no knowledge of pre-existence, nor do we know who we are or where we are going, let us start with Genesis 2 and 3. Judeo-Christian thought is based on the Adam and Eve allegory, which goes back thousands of years to the ancient Babylonian and Chaldean histories. This allegory tells us of man formed out of the dust of the ground and woman taken from Adam's rib. It also explains the way the knowledge of good and evil enters into the mind of man and makes of the mind an arena of conflicting forces, which creates in man the sense of separation and alienation. By beginning our inward journey at this level, we will expose the problem and thus reveal the secret and the solution, for if we fully understand the problem, the solution is clearly seen. "Having eyes, see ye not? and having ears, hear ye not? and do ye not remember?"[8]

The Allegory of Adam and Eve
A Dream Sequence in One Act

The Setting

These are the generations of the heavens and of the earth when they were created, in the day that the Lord God made the earth and the heavens, and every plant of the field before it was in the earth, and every herb of the field before it grew: for the Lord God had not caused it to rain upon the earth, and there was not a man to till the ground. But there went up a mist from the earth, and watered the whole face of the ground. And the Lord God formed man of the dust of the ground, and breathed into his nostrils the breath of life; and man became a living soul. And the Lord God planted a garden eastward in Eden; and there he put the man whom he had formed. And out of the ground made the Lord God to grow every tree that is pleasant to the sight, and good for food; the tree of life also in the midst of the garden, and the tree of knowledge of good and evil. And a river went out of Eden to water the garden; and from thence it was parted, and became into four heads. The name of the first is Pison: that is it which compasseth the whole land of Havilah, where there is gold; and the gold of that land is good: there is bdellium and the onyx stone. And the name of the second river is Gihon: the same is it that compasseth the whole land of Ethiopia. And the name of the third

river is Hiddekel: that is it which goeth toward the east
of Assyria. And the fourth river is Euphrates.

Genesis 2:4–14

The story of creation in Genesis 2 and 3 has
sometimes been called the Adam dream,
because it is an in-depth psychological story of
man falling asleep in the dream of material sense.
It tells of his potential, his disobedience, and his
expulsion from Eden. This story was told around
the family circle as an oral tradition by the ancient
Hebrews of the Middle East.

In those early days the Babylonians, neighbors
of the Hebrews, practiced paganistic prayer and
indulged in sacrifices, both animal and human, as
well as sacred prostitution under Ishtar, their chief
female goddess of sexual love and war. Even
Egypt, which had a strong priesthood and was
known for its science and wisdom schools, wor-
shiped many gods. The Hebrews feared the cor-
rupting influence of these different cultures to their
own morality and monotheism, and so they en-
deavored to keep their religious traditions alive
through the family circle. The storyteller imparted
to the tribe or family a story easily remembered by
the young and a lesson to those who understood
the meaning of the allegory.

The name of God given in the stories of the
Bible indicates the author's degree of enlighten-
ment. Genesis 1 is a mystical view of creation. It
was written much later than Genesis 2 and 3,

probably around 500 BC by Second Isaiah, who
was spoken of as the teacher of righteousness. The
name used for God in the first chapter of Genesis
is *Elohim*. This is the name of the unnameable
One, the Infinite Invisible that maintains and
sustains the universe. No human concept can be
formed of this Deity, for this divine Consciousness
is constantly revealing to us Its divine nature and
character as creation.

The name *Lord God* (Jehovah) of Genesis 2 and
3 is a humanized concept of Deity, which ascribes
human form, personality, and attributes to God.
This humanized concept of Deity is influenced by
man's changing beliefs in good and evil. In the
Adam and Eve story, man has made God in *man's*
image and likeness, knowing both good and evil.
This concept of God exhibits human qualities,
whereas the God of the first chapter of Genesis is
Spirit and cannot be conceptualized.

Our setting opens with "every plant of the field
before it was in the earth, and every herb of the
field before it grew." The allusion to a mist coming
up from the earth suggests that this allegory is a
veil being put over the perfect clear perception of
the Soul-faculties. When we enter the Adam
dream, we are seeing creation as a "mis(t)-con-
ception." Something is obscuring, or veiling, the
truth; something is obscuring man's vision. "For
now we see through a glass, darkly . . . ."[1]

"And the Lord God formed man of the dust of
the ground." In ancient times certain men made

household gods out of clay—fertility gods, rain gods—so it was natural for them to think of God as a potter and man formed out of clay. Job, speaking to God, said, ". . . thou hast made me as the clay; and wilt thou bring me into dust again?"[2] You will notice that the story does not say that the Lord God created man; rather, this man is *formed* out of the dust of the ground. This ground is mind.

Mind forms our human experience, and thought is the clay. The mind can only form and project pictures, or concepts, similar to a motion picture projector. In our dreams we *see* a variety of forms, which are all mind formations. We give the characters in our dreams mental bodies, but when we awaken, the dreamer, the dream, and all its formations disappear. Such a mental picture is being formed for us in this story.

Intelligence is the basic eternal quality of mind enabling us to learn, understand, and reason. Eden signifies "the place of understanding and intellect." (Zohar) Philo said, "Eden is a symbol for correct and divine reason." So we understand the garden of Eden to be a mental garden in which character is developed by the choices made through reason, intellect, and understanding. Early in our human history man was recognized as a mental being; in ancient Greek the word for man and mind was the same, *nous.*

Man is placed in the garden "eastward in Eden." As the light rises from the East, so man's understanding and intellect is receptive to illumination.

Out of this same ground, which we now understand to be mind, unfold many states and stages of consciousness: an awareness of beauty, symbolized by trees that are pleasant to the sight; an awareness of goodness, symbolized by trees that are good for food; the awareness of duality, symbolized by the tree of the knowledge of good and evil; and the awareness and appreciation of eternal Life, symbolized by the Tree of Life.

"A river went out of Eden to water the garden." One stream of life-giving intelligence flows through the mind, communicating through reason, intellect, and understanding. The river flowing out of Eden parts and becomes four rivers, each having a name that reveals an essential activity of mind. Pison is the name of the first river. In Hebrew this means "great outpouring, full-flowing being."[3] This river represents the faculty of *intuition,* through which beauty and goodness are conceived. There is no limit to the immediate apprehension and cognition of direct knowledge revealed through intuition. Intuition is cultivated through contemplation, which prepares the mind for revelation. By learning to trust intuition, man develops self-reliance and self-knowledge.

Havilah, the land through which intuition flows, represents the struggle of elemental life to listen and obey, trusting intuition. This is where virtue is born of trial, the struggle for the good and the true developing the ethical nature of man. This refining process brings out the gold in human character.

Bdellium and onyx symbolize power and wisdom on the moral level.

The name of the second river is Gihon. This symbolizes the formative movement of *perception,* through which we gain knowledge of all things relating to goodness and appreciation of life. Through perception we gain an understanding of our universe and become acquainted with its laws. Observation and appreciation are activities of perception, which lead to clearer conception.

The third river is Hiddekel, which flows toward the east of Assyria. This is the flow of knowledge we receive through the *testimony* of those who have gained knowledge through intuition and direct perception. This allegory is the testimony of early wise men, and through it we learn the ancient psychology of these religious men. As we look at their reasoning processes, our understanding of our religious inheritance is expanded.

The name of the fourth river is Euphrates, which symbolizes the flow of knowledge and understanding gained from the *study of the structural universe.* This includes the animal, vegetable, and mineral kingdoms. This structural sense of the universe, that which we study with our senses, is not spiritual creation but a mortal concept of creation, in which the belief in good and evil is outpictured. Spiritual creation is unseen by our material senses but is ever discernible through our spiritual sense, our mystical awareness.

Cast of Characters

And the Lord God took the man, and put him into the garden of Eden to dress it and to keep it. And the Lord God commanded the man, saying, Of every tree of the garden thou mayest freely eat: but of the tree of the knowledge of good and evil, thou shalt not eat of it: for in the day that thou eatest thereof thou shalt surely die. And the Lord God said, It is not good that the man should be alone; I will make him an help meet for him. And out of the ground the Lord God formed every beast of the field, and every fowl of the air; and brought them unto Adam to see what he would call them: and whatsoever Adam called every living creature, that was the name thereof. And Adam gave names to all cattle, and to the fowl of the air, and to every beast of the field; but for Adam there was not found an help meet for him. And the Lord God caused a deep sleep to fall upon Adam, and he slept: and he took one of his ribs, and closed up the flesh instead thereof; and the rib, which the Lord God had taken from man, made he a woman, and brought her unto the man. And Adam said, This is now bone of my bones, and flesh of my flesh: she shall be called Woman, because she was taken out of Man. Therefore shall a man leave his father and his mother, and shall cleave unto his wife: and they shall be one flesh. And they were both naked, the man and his wife, and were not ashamed.

Genesis 2:15–25

This man of Genesis 2 is a servant, a steward, who is commanded by the Lord God to take care of the garden of Eden. He is to keep his mind filled with appreciation of life, thereby developing his understanding of the beautiful, the good, and the true. He can eat of every tree in the garden except the tree of the knowledge of good and evil. He is warned by the Lord God that he must not eat or partake of the knowledge of good and evil or he will die: he will no longer have singleness of vision and pure understanding. The knowledge of good and evil, once accepted, conditions the mind so that the thinking processes become structured to support these beliefs. The acceptance of these beliefs acts as a universal hypnotism, which clouds our vision and obscures the truth.

In the anthropomorphic sense of God, there is a feeling of separation and loneliness. By naming and labeling all the creatures, Adam builds a psychological and intellectual frame of reference from which to function. Instead of enjoying a oneness with creation as a living soul, he is forming concepts of life, thus making existence a mental experience. When we begin to name and label things, we are classifying and giving each a distinct nature and character. This fosters a sense of separation in us.

In this sense of separation, Adam is lonely. The Lord God causes a deep sleep to fall upon Adam and forms out of his rib a woman. In the deep sleep man thinks he is incomplete without a woman, and woman feels incomplete without a man. At this point in the dream there is no sense of sin or guilt in the mind of Adam and Eve concerning their forms or their relationship to one another.

Scene 1 Disobedience and Guilt

eᵴᵉ

Now the serpent was more subtil than any beast of the field which the Lord God had made. And he said unto the woman, Yea, hath God said, Ye shall not eat of every tree of the garden? And the woman said unto the serpent, We may eat of the fruit of the trees of the garden: but of the fruit of the tree which is in the midst of the garden, God hath said, Ye shall not eat of it, neither shall ye touch it, lest ye die. And the serpent said unto the woman, Ye shall not surely die: for God doth know that in the day ye eat thereof, then your eyes shall be opened, and ye shall be as gods, knowing good and evil. And when the woman saw that the tree was good for food, and that it was pleasant to the eyes, and a tree to be desired to make one wise, she took of the fruit thereof, and did eat, and gave also unto her husband with her; and he did eat. And the eyes of them *Perception* both were opened, and they knew that they were naked; and they sewed fig leaves together, and made themselves aprons. And they heard the voice of the Lord God walking in the garden in the cool of the day: and Adam and his wife hid themselves from the presence of the Lord God amongst the trees of the garden.

Genesis 3:1–8

In many ancient cultures the serpent represented occult wisdom, and sometimes it represented desire and sex. In the dream—for we know that both Adam and Eve are in a deep sleep—a talking serpent (desire) entices Eve into eating the fruit of the tree of the knowledge of good and evil.

As Eve was taken from the rib area of Adam, she represents the emotional nature, so the fruit appeals to her. It appeals to her appetite; it is good for food. It appeals to her aesthetic sense; it is pleasant to her eyes. It appeals to her reason; it is desired to make her wise. So she eats of the fruit and gives it to Adam, who succumbs to desire and thus is disobedient to the Lord God. This particular temptation comes as a suggestion of good, not evil, a suggestion that they will be as gods. The concept that we can add goodness and wisdom to ourselves by accretion instead of unfoldment is materialism and limitation.

The nature of desire is the belief that something outside of ourselves can satisfy our emptiness. Desire always makes us feel that we are lacking something, and with the sense of lack, there is also a sense of fear. Desire, lack, and fear are all part of the sense of separation taking place in the dream.

Because of their disobedience, Adam and Eve now have double vision. Instead of seeing the one Life, they are double-minded, seeing both good and evil forms of life. In their shame they cover their nakedness and hide themselves from the Lord God. The fruits of the tree of the knowledge of good and evil quickly appear as guilt, shame, and fear. How soon the dream of good can turn into the dream of evil! Through desire, Eden, *understanding,* is lost to these two dreamers. Instead of listening to correct, or divine, reasoning, that God had already provided for them every form of

good, they listen to desire and fall more deeply
into sleep. Having adulterated their thinking with $\vee$
the belief in good and evil, they open the way for
universal mental suggestion to operate in human
consciousness.   *hypnotism , race consciousness*

Scene 2 · Punishment and the Curse

And the Lord God called unto Adam, and said unto
him, Where art thou? And he said, I heard thy voice in
the garden, and I was afraid, because I was naked; and
I hid myself. And he said, Who told thee that thou wast   ?
naked? Hast thou eaten of the tree, whereof I commanded thee that thou shouldest not eat? And the man
said, The woman whom thou gavest to be with me, she
gave me of the tree, and I did eat. And the Lord God
said unto the woman, What is this that thou hast done?
And the woman said, The serpent beguiled me, and I
did eat. And the Lord God said unto the serpent,
Because thou hast done this, thou art cursed above all
cattle, and above every beast of the field; upon thy
belly shalt thou go, and dust shalt thou eat all the days
of thy life: and I will put enmity between thee and the
woman, and between thy seed and her seed; it shall
bruise thy head, and thou shalt bruise his heel. Unto
the woman he said, I will greatly multiply thy sorrow
and thy conception; in sorrow thou shalt bring forth
children; and thy desire shall be to thy husband, and he
shall rule over thee. And unto Adam he said, Because
thou hast hearkened unto the voice of thy wife, and
hast eaten of the tree, of which I commanded thee,
saying, Thou shalt not eat of it: cursed is the ground for
thy sake; in sorrow shalt thou eat of it all the days of thy

life; thorns also and thistles shall it bring forth to thee; and thou shalt eat the herb of the field; in the sweat of thy face shalt thou eat bread, till thou return unto the ground; for out of it wast thou taken: for dust thou art, and unto dust shalt thou return.

Genesis 3:9–19

When Adam is asked if he has eaten the fruit of the tree of the knowledge of good and evil, he blames Eve, who blames the serpent. This is the first "passing of the buck." Eve admits her act, blaming the impersonal temptation called the serpent, ". . . that old serpent, called the Devil, and Satan, which deceiveth the whole world . . . ."[4]

Thus a curse is put on man and woman by the Lord God, a god who rewards and punishes, who blesses and curses. In this dream world Adam and Eve live under condemnation. Both childbearing and work are filled with sorrow and suffering. This dream formation cannot be spiritualized. It can only disappear into its native nothingness as awakening takes place, for the dreamer and the dream are one.

Scene 3 - Expulsion and Separation

And Adam called his wife's name Eve; because she was the mother of all living. Unto Adam also and to his wife did the Lord God make coats of skin, and clothed them. And the Lord God said, Behold, the man is become as one of us, to know good and evil: and now,

lest he put forth his hand, and take also of the tree of
life, and eat, and live for ever: therefore the Lord God
sent him forth from the garden of Eden, to till the
ground from whence he was taken. So he drove out the
man; and he placed at the east of the garden of Eden
Cherubims, and a flaming sword which turned every
way, to keep the way of the tree of life.

Genesis 3:20–24

In Hebrew, Eve means *elemental living,* which
indicates that in the dream of material sense,
Adam and Eve are living at the elemental level of
life. They are not clothed in their rightful mind,
because they are asleep in the belief, or dream, of
two powers. This belief of duality clothes them
with a material sense of body.

Today's society still puts great emphasis on
sensuality–sex, money, and fame–which drives
man at the elemental level of life. The evolution of
religious consciousness demands that man tran-
scend his sensuality, making this area of his experience secondary to the great flow of intuition and
spiritual understanding, thereby opening the very
floodgates of heaven. Life, including all relationships, is then experienced in higher ways of love
and understanding.

And so, the characters in the dream, Adam and
Eve, are driven out of Eden by desire and disobedience. Spiritual innocence is forgotten, and the
direct way to Eden is barred, only to be gained
through the struggle to awaken. Now, like Jacob,
man must wrestle with the angel until his nature

changes from being a warrior to being a peace-maker, from self-preservation to brotherly love. The real Self stands at the door knocking, waiting for the seekers of Light to open the door so that they may eat of the Tree of Life.

The real Self is revealed in the east where the Sun of Righteousness shines forth. Here stands the cherubim, the watcher or sentinel, who is awake. The "flaming sword" is the Word of God, which is imparted to the awakened understanding. "For the word of God is quick [living], and powerful, and sharper than any two-edged sword, piercing even to the dividing asunder of soul and spirit, and of the joints and marrow, and is a discerner of the thoughts and intents of the heart."[5]

The Two Trees

When the Master stood before Pilate, who represented the greatest temporal power on earth in his day, he said, ". . . My kingdom is not of this world: if my kingdom were of this world, then would my servants fight . . ."[1] To me, the Tree of Life and the tree of the knowledge of good and evil signify "My kingdom" and "this world."

If we consider "My kingdom" as a spiritual dimension governed by grace and truth, we can see that this corresponds to Genesis 1, which discloses the oneness of God, man, and universe. That which the Master called "this world" corresponds to the Adam dream of Genesis 2 and 3, the mental realm that is conditioned by the belief in good and evil, making this realm an arena of conflicting forces.

The two trees in the garden of Eden symbolize these two very different levels of awareness. As a branch on the tree of the knowledge of good and evil, we are dependent on what we know. As a branch on the Tree of Life, we are dependent on Who we know, Whose wisdom is infinite, enlightening the mind and filling the soul with peace.

As we look more deeply into these creation myths, we see that the goal of our whole earthly existence is to awaken from the Adam dream of

21

"this world" to the awareness of being children of God, who live in "My kingdom" and are governed by the everlasting Father, the Prince of Peace.

The Tree of the Knowledge of Good and Evil

"Hear ye indeed, but understand not; and see ye indeed, but perceive not."

Isaiah 6:9

The tree of the knowledge of good and evil is the dream scene, the world of human concepts in which we struggle with the pairs of opposites, the pains and pleasures of material sense, never realizing that we are making our own dream in accordance with our ignorance of spiritual principles. As the dreamer, we have forgotten our Eden experience, and therefore, our spiritual understanding is dormant. We are immersed in the fears and desires of the flesh. We are not under the law, protection, or sustaining power of God, but are experiencing the human beliefs that we accept as true. The believer and the belief are one, just as the dreamer and the dream are one.

The tree of the knowledge of good and evil is the family tree of the human race. Every tribe, clan, and race are branches on that tree, each branch having all the mores, beliefs, and opinions of that group. There is no true individuality on this tree; each person reacts according to the group with which he is identified, having all the characteristics of his group and coming under the material and mental laws operating on this family tree. He is not a seeker after truth but, rather, a believer and a follower of the knowledge of good and evil.

Subliminal hypnotic suggestions permeate the atmosphere of the human scene, making it an arena for conflicting forces. All these suggestions, or concepts, are the outpicturing of the belief in good and evil, which enters the one universal mind, conditioning it by the pairs of opposites: health and sickness, desire and fear, love and hate, wealth and poverty, war and peace, birth and death, success and failure. We ourselves are not responsible for this conditioning; it was here when we entered the human scene. The conditioned mind disclosed in the second chapter of Genesis has been operating subliminally throughout the ages in the human psyche, mentally forming a limited, selfish, world viewpoint with which mortals identify. This universal hypnotism is the fabricator of all our problems.

As part of the human race, concerned with self-preservation on this family tree, we are captives without choice. We think we have a choice and try to choose good over evil, right over wrong, but we really are captives of our human concepts and of the hypnotic atmosphere surrounding us. In this atmosphere of mental suggestion, the personal self, feeling dissatisfaction, distress, and unfulfillment, tries to fill its personal sense of existence by

to get things out

struggling to achieve, accumulate, and possess through personal power.

The tree of the knowledge of good and evil is symbolized by a deciduous tree, such as an apple or a fig tree. A deciduous tree goes through cycles of change and seasons. It is acted upon by climate, being in a state of constant change. In spring, it grows and blossoms; in summer, it bears fruit; in the fall, it loses its leaves; in winter, it is dormant. The next spring, the cycle begins again as the tree renews itself from the "death-like" dormant stage.

For a deciduous tree one year, a complete cycle, is a parenthesis in time. Likewise, every member of the human race lives within a parenthesis imposed on the circle of eternal Life.[2] This parenthesis is the period from birth to the grave. When we accept birth as the beginning of our life, then we accept death as the end. All who are attached to the tree of the knowledge of good and evil are living within a parenthesis from the time they are born until they die, and they will experience parenthesis after parenthesis until they are awakened from the dream.

> "For, behold, the darkness shall cover the earth,
>   and gross darkness the people:
> But the Lord shall arise upon thee,
>   and his glory shall be seen upon thee.
> And the Gentiles shall come to thy light,
>   and kings to the brightness of thy rising."
>   Isaiah 60:2–3

The Tree of Life

Arise, shine; for thy light is come, and the glory of the Lord is risen upon thee.

Isaiah 60:1

The Tree of Life is symbolized by an evergreen tree, such as the Christmas tree. The evergreen does not react to conditions of chance and change as does the deciduous tree. It continually grows new needles or leaves before shedding the old ones. Some evergreens, such as the sequoias, live for thousands of years and thus symbolize eternal life. Life is continually renewing itself as the life of the tree, which is the life of the seed, which is the life of the tree, eternally unfolding as spiritual creation. In this creation there is only one life, one substance, one activity, one power, and this One is Spirit, God.

Just as the Christmas tree symbolizes the coming of the Christ, or Messiah, to human consciousness, revealing the real Self, so the Tree of Life is the symbol for My kingdom, the spiritual world of God's government. As we seek the Son, we awaken from the dream, for it is through the Son that we experience God's government.

"For unto us a child is born,
  unto us a son is given:
And his name shall be called
  Wonderful, Counsellor, The mighty God,
  The everlasting Father, The Prince of Peace.

Of the increase of his government and peace
    there shall be no end,
Upon the throne of David,
    and upon his kingdom,
To order it, and to establish it
    with judgment and with justice
    from henceforth even for ever.
The zeal of the Lord of hosts will perform this."

Isaiah 9:6–7

The Tree of Life is the family tree of the children of God, the hierarchy of heaven, including all the saints, sages, and seers who have gone before us. The awakened being lives in the circle of eternal Life, not in a parenthesis imposed on that circle. The Tree of Life is the consciousness of Oneness, the world that mystics throughout all ages have revealed. In this consciousness of eternal Life, the Son is forever operating harmoniously, maintaining and sustaining spiritual creation in all its integrity.

"For by him were all things created,
    that are in heaven, and that are in earth,
    visible and invisible,
Whether they be thrones, or dominions,
    or principalities, or powers:
All things were created by him, and for him:
    and he is before all things,
    and by him all things consist."

Colossians 1:16–17

Rousing the Dormant Understanding

"Cease ye from man, whose breath is in his nostrils:
for wherein is he to be accounted of?"

Isaiah 2:22

How do we disconnect ourselves from the tree of the knowledge of good and evil and find our way back to divine Consciousness, the Tree of Life? How do we bring ourselves under His government? What are the spiritual principles revealed in these two Genesis stories of creation?

"Come now, and let us reason together,
    saith the Lord:
Though your sins be as scarlet,
    they shall be as white as snow. . . .
If ye be willing and obedient,
    ye shall eat the good of the land."

Isaiah 1:18–19

The allegory of Adam and Eve is based on the belief of a selfhood separate and apart from God and a belief in two powers, good and evil. At this level of awareness, we are praying up to a god, that anthropomorphic sense of God whom man has made in man's image and likeness. Since we believe this God to be a rewarding and punishing God, a giving and withholding God, we are begging and beseeching Him to give, to reward, and we are fearful lest He punish or withhold.

If we believe in the evidence of our physical senses and either consciously or unknowingly

28 ~ Genesis

accept into our mind the belief of an imperfect world, we feel compelled to instruct God. Thus in our prayer we try to influence God, sometimes even through sacrifice, to change the conditions of the world.

But "this world" is not the world of God's creating; it is a misconception of the real and eternal world, which is here and now. Therefore, our prayers are founded on a lie, and we are praying amiss. The solution to the problem cannot be found at the level of the problem by praying to God to correct the mistakes of this dream world. We must awaken to the fallacy of this world picture by consciously opening our mind to the Truth and thus being taught of the Spirit.

Our prayer then is:

Father, let me see the world as You see it.
Open my spiritual ears, open my spiritual eyes,
that I may see creation as You see it.

> "For my thoughts are not your thoughts,
> Neither are your ways my ways,
>   saith the Lord.
> For as the heavens are higher than the earth,
>   so are my ways higher than your ways,
>   and my thoughts than your thoughts."
>   Isaiah 55:8–9

The Door

"Behold, I stand at the door, and knock . . . ."
                                Revelation 3:20

unfolding

Creation is not a historical event taking place in time and space. It is the unfolding of divine Consciousness eternally now and completely spontaneous. It is the dawning in individual awareness of the infinite nature and character of God, Who reveals heaven on earth. Through our recognition of spiritual principles and the Presence within, a door is opened to us.

This door to the Light is formed by the building blocks of spiritual understanding as revealed in Genesis 1 in the seven days of creation. As we understand the spiritual meaning of these seven days, we walk through the darkness of human misconceptions into the dawn of a new day, finally realizing what the Master, Christ Jesus, meant when he said, "I am the door: by me if any man enter in, he shall be saved, and shall go in and out, and find pasture."[3] Jesus knew the spiritual principle of Oneness, as revealed in Genesis 1. This consciousness of Truth/Love is the door by which each of us walks into the light of a new day of spiritual understanding and a higher altitude of prayer.

The Call to Awake

"Ho, every one that thirsteth, come ye to the waters,
And he that hath no money; come ye, buy, and eat;
Yea, come, buy wine and milk
Without money and without price.

Wherefore do ye spend money for that which is not bread? and your labour for that which satisfieth not?

Hearken diligently unto me, and eat ye that which is good, and let your soul delight itself in fatness. [fulness]

Incline your ear, and come unto me:
Hear, and your soul shall live;
And I will make an everlasting covenant with you,
Even the sure mercies of David. [grace]"

Isaiah 55:1–3

Part II
Fulfillment

The First Day...

Awakening

In the beginning God created the heaven and the earth. And the earth was without form, and void; and darkness was upon the face of the deep. And the Spirit of God moved upon the face of the waters. And God said, Let there be light: and there was light. And God saw the light, that it was good: and God divided the light from the darkness. And God called the light Day, and the darkness he called Night. And the evening and the morning were the first day.

Genesis 1:1–5

Creation is the activity of divine Principle revealing eternal Life in an infinite way. Spiritually speaking, there is no beginning and no ending in creation. The Latin Vulgate translation of the Bible begins Genesis in this way: "In *principle,* God created the heaven and the earth." Life, Spirit, is eternally manifesting Itself as incorporeal heaven and earth. With our awakening understanding we see the light and know that there is a divine Principle revealing Itself as "heaven and earth."

The spiritual sense of the word *heaven* is the consciousness of harmony and peace, maintained by Spirit. The spiritual sense of the word *earth* is this heavenly consciousness of Light and Love manifesting as spiritual ideas. Thus, Heaven and earth are one, as Principle and Its ideas are one, and It is good.

As we seek a clearer view of creation unfolding as Consciousness, we close our eyes in meditation and face the darkness within. As yet, the spiritual ideas are unformed in our awareness, so that we see and hear nothing. There is only a void, a vacuum. Even though we may hesitate to enter this dark womb of silence, we must, if we are to understand the kingdom of God, for within this darkness the Spirit of God moves.

When Jesus said to his disciples, ". . . Launch out into the deep, and let down your nets for a draught,"[1] he was instructing us to probe the depths of our being in order to catch the multitude of spiritual ideas. These unseen but ever available ideas are waiting to be brought forth to our conscious awareness. Patiently searching the deep withinness of our being is a form of creative meditation through which we enter the kingdom of God. We are becoming aware of a reality that cannot be defined; we are drawing upon intuition, which is greater than our physical senses and human faculties of reason. This new awareness is the beginning of spiritual sense, the first dawning of the light of a new day.

"And the light shineth in darkness; and the darkness comprehended it not."[2] A darkened understanding is one that is ignorant of the spiritual

Presence. Since Truth is omnipresent, there can be no absence of Truth; darkness is but a temporary lapse in awareness of our original state of being. When there seems to be no spiritual activity, this is our night, but we are resting and waiting patiently for the day, or light. Day is when the Spirit is active in us, revealing and illuminating the truth of Being. We are awakening from the dream of a material sense of existence into the spiritual sense of creation. At this point in our unfoldment we are "the people that walked in darkness [and] have seen a great light . . . ."[3] This is the first day of My kingdom.

Living in the First Day

[handwritten marginal note: learning to be present, to be now]

". . . Awake thou that sleepest, and arise from the dead, and Christ shall give thee light."

Ephesians 5:14

Whether we are aware of it or not, what is, *is.* The activity of God, Light, is expressing Itself in the only way that It can, universally and impersonally as Love. This means that Love is equally available to everyone. However, there is nothing we can do to deserve it; ". . . he maketh his sun to rise on the evil and on the good, and sendeth rain on the just and on the unjust."[4] Universal, impersonal Love is pouring Itself forth to each of us as grace, and we receive as much as we can accept. We only need to be humble enough to turn within and be still to find the kingdom of heaven.

On our first day of creation we begin to turn away from a personal sense of ego. We are touched by the grace of God, thus awakening from the dream and willing to be led of the Spirit. The Greek word for repentance is *metanoia,* which means turning with the mind. We are turning with the mind to the silence within, focusing on the unseen presence of God instead of on the world of effect and thus giving it power.

Repentance, of course, is not a one-time activity. During this awakening stage of unfolding consciousness, there will be many instances when we realize that we have slipped back into the dream and are accepting the universal belief in two powers. Then we again quickly repent, without indulging in self-condemnation, and ask for forgiveness for looking outward, thereby erasing the false concept we have formed. Through repentance and forgiveness, we consciously disconnect ourselves from the discordant world of material sense and consciously identify with the kingdom of God within us. Now we are ready to receive the healing and transforming power of Love.

Even though we may not always feel the presence of God, we must consciously acknowledge God's omnipresence in every act. This we call practicing the presence of God.[5] At first this is a mental act. From the moment we get up in the morning we acknowledge:

"This is the day which God hath made."[6] God is the light unto this day. In this day there is no darkness of

two powers; there is only the all-presence and all-power
of the light of Love. The light of Love shines in this
day, illuminating the way. I will rejoice and be glad in
it. Love is unfolding Its plan for this day. Love directs,
protects, and guides me every step of the way, and I
will listen for Love's voice today.*

We follow this acknowledgment with a minute
or two of inner silence and receptivity to the Spirit,
for it is the inner Presence, the Spirit, that effects
the change in us.

Throughout each day we must consciously and
constantly continue short prayers of acknowledgment. If we find ourselves going through long
periods without remembering to acknowledge the
presence of God, we might set a timer for fif-
teen-minute intervals to "awaken" us. This re-
minder will establish the habit of practicing the
Presence. Eventually, Consciousness will take
over, and we will receive impetus from within.
Then, as we follow every acknowledgment with a
moment of silence for listening, we gradually begin
to feel the presence of "My peace."

Maintaining an attitude of receptivity and
listening is living in the Now.[7] The only way we
can live in the Light is to live in the now moment.
This takes great mental alertness and acuity at this
stage of unfoldment, because we so easily return to
the past with regrets or we project into the future
with fear or desire, thereby entering the dream.

---

* Meditations are examples of unfoldments, not formulas.

*will not doing own!
it's our own!
Trust + Faith*

But still, the Spirit working in us enables us to continue to practice, to forgive our forgetting and return to the Now.

✗ In *The Gospel According to Thomas,*[8] Jesus said to his disciples, "If they ask you what is the sign of your Father in you, say unto them it is a movement and a rest." As we keep turning within to the Light, there is a movement in consciousness, the God-activity of quietness, and there is also a resting in it. The awareness of this inner peace and poise is probably the first clue that something spiritual is transpiring.

The seeds of truth that we contemplate imbue our mind and grow in us, expanding our awareness from the material state to the spiritual. In contemplative meditation we remind ourselves of ✗ the omnipresence of God's grace, which is already present where we are, regardless of outward appearances:

The Light within me shines, and it is good. I am awakening to this new day of Light and Love. Love reigns supreme. Love forgives my mistakes and guides me into inner peace.

Then we rest in stillness, listening for His Word, that silent assurance, and letting the Light within shine forth to dispel the darkness of misconceptions and misunderstanding.

"In returning and rest shall ye be saved; in quietness and confidence shall be your strength."

Isaiah 30:15

The Second Day. . .

Spiritual Discernment

And God said, Let there be a firmament in the midst of
the waters and let it divide the waters from the waters.
And God made the firmament, and divided the waters
which were under the firmament from the waters which
were above the firmament: and it was so. And God
called the firmament Heaven. And the evening and the
morning were the second day.

Genesis 1:6–8

The spiritual meaning of the word *firmament*
is expansion. Our creative meditations are
no longer "without form and void." We are aware of
increased alertness, new strength and vigor, keener
perception of any interior movement in Consciousness. We are gaining a firm understanding of the
difference between *above* and *below, within* and
without. We begin to understand the statement, ". . .
the kingdom of God is within you"[1]: not within the
body but within our awareness, for the finite can   *extension*
never contain the infinite. We call this expansion of
awareness *spiritual discernment,* the dividing line
between the realized Truth and the letter of truth.

We begin creative meditation by taking into our
awareness the word of God from Scripture, pondering

it, and thus expanding our understanding of a specific truth. This mental act of contemplating the word of God corresponds to "the waters which were under the firmament."

The thoughts and intentions that come from human experience can be good or bad. Even our good intentions often bring bad results, because our human mentality is limited and still filled with the belief in two powers. Paul saw this in himself when he said, "For the good that I would I do not: but the evil which I would not, that I do."[2] At this point Paul had only the letter of truth, "the waters which were under the firmament." He was not functioning in the spirit of Truth, "the waters which were above the firmament," until he was awake and aware, spiritually discerning ". . . I live; yet not I, but Christ liveth in me. . . ."[3]

The "waters below" is the pondering of the letter of truth to purify and expand our limited mentality. The "waters above" is the spontaneous and inspirational Word that utters Itself. This is the water that Jesus referred to when he said, ". . . whosoever drinketh of the water that I shall give him shall never thirst; but the water that I shall give him shall be in him a well of water springing up into everlasting life."[4]

As you can see, we can use the mind in two ways: to formulate concepts, proving mind's utility on the reasoning level, or to turn inward with the mind to the spiritual kingdom, letting it be an avenue of awareness for spiritual ideas. When we go beyond the mental realm of contemplation to a state of receptivity, the Word of God comes to us from within our own being and gives us the spiritual discernment to perceive the difference be- *insights* tween the letter of truth and the spirit of Truth.

During the second day of unfoldment we are given the spiritual discernment to understand the difference between a temporal, changing, mental concept and spiritual Reality. Through spiritual discernment, or what Shankara called "the Crest-jewel of discrimination," heaven is revealed to us, enabling us to live in harmony here and now.

"For, behold, I create new heavens and a new earth: and the former things shall not be remembered, nor come into mind."[5] — *forgiveness*

Living in the Second Day

"So shall my word be that goeth forth out of my mouth: it shall not return unto me void, but it shall accomplish that which I please. . . ."

Isaiah 55:11

At this level of unfoldment we are beginning to realize what is meant by living between two worlds: the world of a material sense of existence, the Adam dream, with all its duality impinging upon our awareness, and the vision that is being presented to us in Genesis 1 of My kingdom, God's creation.

A materialist says that reality is that which is based on the evidence of the five physical senses.

A scientist might say that reality is the mental law behind what one can touch, taste, hear, smell, and see. But those with spiritual discernment know that Reality is that which supports the law that enables the form to appear. Spiritual discernment allows us to look through every appearance to the underlying Reality. This is one of the ways that the human mind is educated out of drawing conclusions from the observations of the senses alone, or even from the scientific deductions based on a structural sense of the world.

Now that we are aware of spiritual discernment, we can be "in the world but not of it." We can enter the mental realm and utilize the mind, which is a beautiful instrument for this world's needs. But we must stay awake and refrain from judging by appearances, for underlying any appearance is the spiritual Reality awaiting our recognition. We must make constant adjustments within ourselves, letting go of misconceptions, rejecting all beliefs in a power and presence apart from God. In this way the spiritual sense of earth and its infinite manifestations is recognized and rightly identified and becomes more real to us.

With even a measure of spiritual discernment, we have a choice. As we look with our expanded awareness of Spirit and Its formations, we see that we have been classifying everyone and everything as attached to the tree of the knowledge of good and evil. Now we can consciously choose to break this attachment by realizing:

Help me to see this differently

Acim

I choose to see this world differently. I choose to see only God and His infinite manifestations. I choose to see everyone as attached to the Tree of Life, fed by His love, walking in the Light.

This willingness to choose to see our world from a spiritual viewpoint is an important step in prayer.

Jesus said to his disciples, "Ye are the salt of the earth . . .",[6] inferring that those who know the truth are a purifying influence to all mankind. Reinterpretation acts as the "salt," the purifying agent that rules out of human consciousness universal false beliefs. We, too, are children of Light, knowing the truth that makes us free. As we stay constantly aware of the divine nature of God as Omniscience, Omnipotence, and Omnipresence, we begin to understand that the Reality of every individual is unseen to material sense and is discernible only to spiritual sense. Although we can never completely free our mind from mistaken concepts through reinterpretation, this does prepare the way for the Word of God until, through spiritual discernment and revelation, we realize: "Oh, yes! God is not in the appearance; He is the inner Being, the Tree of Life."

"Happy is the man that findeth wisdom,
      and the man that getteth understanding. . . .
She is more precious than rubies:
      and all things thou canst desire
      are not to be compared unto her.
Length of days is in her right hand;
      and in her left hand riches and honor.

> Her ways are ways of pleasantness,
> and all her paths are peace.
> She is a tree of life to them that
> lay hold upon her: and happy
> is every one that retaineth her."
>
> Proverbs 3:13, 15–18

If we live at the level of the Adam dream, as a branch connected to the tree of the knowledge of good and evil, then we are seeing people as branches on that same tree. Functioning from a materially structured viewpoint, we view others as part of this same framework. But with spiritual discernment, we have a clearer view of creation and live on a higher level of conscious awareness. At this level we see ourselves and others as *one* with the Tree of Life, spiritual Consciousness.

This unfoldment of Consciousness is exemplified in the story of Jesus and the blind man.[7] Jesus asked him, "Do you see anything?" And the man replied, "I see men, but they look like trees, walking." Then again Jesus touched him, and the man looked intently and was restored, seeing everything clearly. The Master had opened his mystical awareness to see the grand design of the Trinity, which is the Tree of Life: branches, trunk, roots.

As we catch a vision of this truth of Being, oh, how we love it! We love to be told of the way of grace, of God's love and perfection, and of our spiritual identity and wholeness as one with the Tree of Life. But putting the principles into practice requires great mental alertness, and often we

forget, which makes the practice difficult. We
fluctuate between the two trees, these two levels of
awareness, until the loving touch of the Son clears
our vision completely so that we see only eternal
Life in manifestation.

It is revealed to us in Genesis 1 that there is
only one power, one substance, and one activity,
and that One is God. Creation is the activity of
Spirit, Love, expressing and revealing Itself as
incorporeal being and universe. The Principle is
perfect; the spiritual ideas of creation are perfect
and eternal. Spiritual discernment reveals that God
expresses as man, including the universe; therefore, there is nothing and no one to be healed.

In our contemplative prayer work, we correct
our viewpoint, much like focusing the lens of a
camera to get a clear picture. There is no place
where error exists except as an out-of-focus picture
in the unillumined mind. The person who believes
in any power or presence separate and apart from
God is tuning into this distorted view, so the contemplation or adjustment is made in the one mind
by letting in the light of Truth/Love. We adjust our
thinking by always contemplating the principles of
the nature of God as omnipresent Truth/Love and
the nature of individual being as the manifestation
of this Reality, thus bringing into focus that which
truly is, just as Jesus did with the blind man.

As we become aware of our true identity as
God created us, we no longer identify with the
material, or personal, sense of body. The Light

within us enables us to relinquish the sense of personal good and personal evil. As we recognize the impersonal nature of the belief in a power and presence apart from the one Life, which God is, the limited sense of being disappears.

We now have the spiritual discernment to lay the axe at the root of the tree of the knowledge of good and evil, completely detaching ourselves and others from this tree by understanding that any evil coming into our lives is not personal to us. All erroneous conditions are the impersonal belief in two powers operating as a universal hypnotism. We are not to blame ourselves for the error, nor are we to blame anyone else. However, we are responsible for knowing this principle of impersonalization and consciously applying it to every situation.

Likewise, we do not take credit for the good that manifests through us, because all good is the grace of God appearing in a visible and tangible way as we identify with the Tree of Life. The Master said, ". . . Why callest thou me good? there is none good but one, that is, God."[8] This universal goodness is an inherent quality of spiritual Creation, which expresses Itself only as good.

After impersonalizing error of any kind, we must nothingize any appearance of evil by knowing that it has no God-given power or authority. We dismiss all human concepts and appearances by consciously withdrawing power from them. This is another purifying activity of illumination that prepares the mind to receive the truth of harmonious being.

Let us contemplate the subject of body. If we are functioning from the level of two powers, then our body is functioning in an atmosphere of conflict, responding to the false concepts we hold in our mind. For instance, as long as we have a picture of disease in our mind, for ourselves or others, we are accepting that concept. That which appears as a sick or sinning body is the erroneous, out-of-focus concept that we entertain in our mentality.

But spiritual discernment reveals to us that, behind the human concept of body formed by the knowledge of good and evil, there is the spiritual idea created by God, the Tree of Life. Life is Spirit, and all the manifestations of Life are spiritual and incorruptible. When we have the spiritual discernment to recognize the Godhead as the Tree of Life, including branches, trunk, and roots, we free ourselves of the false concept of body. Since the belief in evil has no God-given power to maintain and sustain erroneous concepts, we can release the false view from our thought, knowing that the integrity of the Tree of Life is intact. Thus we bring into focus the divine idea of the Trinity.

Mind, as an instrument for God, is infinite, pure, and unconditioned,[9] unless we introduce into it the belief in good and evil. When we do not condition our mind by judging after appearances, then our mind, in that holy instant of Nowness, reveals a more perfect concept. We reconcile man to God as we witness the truth.

"Ye are my witnesses, saith the Lord,
    and my servant whom I have chosen:

That ye may know and believe me,
    and understand that I am he:
Before me there was no God formed,
Neither shall there be after me.
I, even I, am the Lord;
    and beside me there is no saviour."

Isaiah 43:10

With spiritual discernment there is no need to ask God for anything in this world. "But seek ye first the kingdom of God, and his righteousness; and all these things shall be added unto you."[10] We ask only that our mind be purified and brought into focus to see more and more of Love's revelation as we yield ourselves to the divine Will. Our prayer might be:

Thank you, Father, for showing me that there is a difference between this world and My kingdom. Now I have a choice; I choose to let the light of Love dispel the illusions of sense to reveal only the purity of your creation. I wait for that "gentle sound of stillness."

"And the spirit of the Lord shall rest upon him,
    the spirit of wisdom and understanding,
    the spirit of counsel and might,
    the spirit of knowledge
    and of the fear [awe] of the Lord. . . .
And he shall not judge after the sight of his eyes,
Neither reprove after the hearing of his ears."

Isaiah 11:2–3

The Third Day . . .

Opening of the Soul Center

And God said, Let the waters under the heaven be gathered together unto one place, and let the dry land appear: and it was so. And God called the dry land Earth; and the gathering together of the waters called he Seas: and God saw that it was good. And God said, Let the earth bring forth grass, the herb yielding seed, and the fruit tree yielding fruit after his kind, whose seed is in itself, upon the earth: and it was so. And the earth brought forth grass, and herb yielding seed after his kind, and the tree yielding fruit, whose seed was in itself, after his kind: and God saw that it was good. And the evening and the morning were the third day.

Genesis 1:9–13

Dry land is the symbol for Soul. It is the holy ground upon which we stand, where growth, or spiritual unfoldment, takes place. This is the holy ground that Moses stood on when God revealed His name as ". . . I AM THAT I AM."[1] It is the same holy ground that Isaiah stood on when God spoke to him and said, "I am the first, and I am the last; and beside me there is no God,"[2] thus disclosing the infinite realm of Soul that functions as the law of unfolding good.

The Soul center must be opened in us before we can experience our oneness with God and with all spiritual being and idea, because it is in Soul that every spiritual faculty is active and every spiritual idea is embodied. This spiritual center in us is like the bud of a rose, which only sunlight can open. In meditation we are in His light, and Love is refracted through the crystal loveliness of Soul, revealing to our mystical awareness the beauty of Holiness. The dry land appears as fertile ground for every attribute of Love to grow in us.

For our spiritual unfoldment it is important for us to understand the facets of God known as Soul and Spirit. Spirit is the invisible substance, activity, and power of God, while Soul is the purity, the "womb of silence," through which we experience God and all spiritual creation. In creative meditation we function *in* Soul and *as* Soul. Mary, inspired by the angel of the Lord, said, ". . . My soul doth magnify the Lord."[3] She was praying spiritually and sincerely, opening the way for the Son of God to appear. In this purity of Soul, the immaculate conception took place through the power of the Spirit. This is the mystical union that awaits us in meditation. We wait in the holy stillness of Soul so that the spiritual idea of Sonship may unfold in us. "Behold, a virgin shall conceive, and bear a son, and shall call his name Immanuel [God-with-us]."[4]

The truths that we ponder, called the "living waters," are now gathered together into an ocean of consciousness. Just as the ocean supports the

smallest to the largest ships, so does Soul-conscious-
ness support the smallest to the greatest spiritual
ideas. On the third day of spiritual unfoldment, a
definite movement in consciousness through Soul-
awareness is taking place, and the Word of God is
supporting this new expression of creation.

Grass symbolizes both humility and resilience.
It is the simplest of forms and yet, when walked
upon, it springs back unharmed. It can grow
through the smallest crack in concrete and break
it open. When we turn inward in meditation with
humility, the seed of God grows in us, and we are
filled with peace and joy. We discover that this
prayerful attitude of humility will gently break
through every barrier that would hide our good,
revealing the infinite resources of Soul. Jesus'
humility made him mighty, for in his denial of his
human self, the God-self appeared. "I can of mine
own self do nothing[5] . . . the Father that dwelleth
in me, he doeth the works."[6]

Spirit yields spiritual seeds, seeds of Truth and
Love. These seeds are planted in holy ground, the
Soul, and they grow by grace as consciousness
unfolds. The holy ground, the Soul, is the good
ground that Jesus speaks of in the parable of the
sower sowing his seed in different types of soil.[7]
The seed, the Word of God, that is planted by the
wayside meets with too much resistance from
material sense. The seed that is planted on stony
ground has no root, so there is no endurance in
times of trouble. The seed that is planted among

thorns is choked by the cares of this world and the desire for possessions. But the Word of God that is planted in humility springs up and bears fruit richly.

The fruit tree yielding fruit after his kind, whose seed is in itself, reveals spiritual law. It is an absolute necessity to have a consciousness of this spiritual law of like begetting like. In the material sense of creation we have the law of cause and effect, or karma. This so-called law is based on evidence from the five physical senses, not on Truth. In spiritual creation there is only one law, because there is only one substance and one Source. God is both cause and effect; Spirit can only beget Spirit. God is begetting Himself as creation; therefore, each spiritual expression is fulfilling itself from within itself in spiritual integrity.

When Jesus' disciples asked him, ". . . Master, who did sin, this man, or his parents, that he was born blind?",[8] Jesus' reply, that neither the man nor his parents sinned, unequivocally corrects the error of a belief in karma or any personal cause. This particular teaching of Jesus gave me great comfort, surety, and help in healing once when my young son was troubled by an appearance of ugly growths on his foot. I had called a practitioner for help, but she immediately began probing the probability of a mental cause stemming from my son's or my own erroneous thoughts or feelings.

Knowing within that this approach was inconsistent with the omnipotence of God, I quickly ended the conversation. Then, opening my Bible

for guidance, I was given the above passage. In
agreement and gratitude I released all concern for
the persistent appearance, and within a few min-
utes the foot was completely healed. As I focused
on the fact that God is expressing Himself as
individual spiritual integrity, that cause and effect
are one, I was released.

A law is only as effective as its enforcing
agency. Since God is that which is enforcing and
upholding spiritual law, we know that spiritual
creation is all good, being maintained and sustained by spiritual law. The Seed, the Word of
God, is in Itself, fulfilling Itself as the kingdom of
God on earth. Fruitage appears from our meditations and prayer according to the depth of our
realization of God's spiritual law. God-seed is in
us, begetting Itself, and, therefore, we can only
grow in grace and truth.

The visible expressions of Life are concepts,
holographic pictures or reflections of the invisible,
perfect, spiritual ideas of Soul. Human concepts
appear to change and evolve, but spiritual ideas,
such as body, home, relationships, supply, and
government are immortal, eternal, incorruptible,
and unchanging. These spiritual ideas are forever
fixed in Soul. As we ponder and contemplate the
spiritual ideas, they expand and take on new and
more gracious expressions. God expresses everything out of His own infinite goodness; all creation
functions by the law of God.

Living in the Third Day

". . . And their soul shall be as a watered garden;
and they shall not sorrow any more at all."

Jeremiah 31:12

Every perfect gift of God is in our soul, waiting
for us to turn within and draw upon it. It is in our
soul that the Son of God is revealed to us and gives
My peace. It is in the purity of Soul that My joy
comes, the joy that no man can take away. My
peace and My joy are the perfume of the Soul, the
essence of divine Sonship-consciousness. Oh, the
soul of man is God; the soul of man is His spiritual
temple, a "temple . . . made without hands,"
eternal in the heavens.[9] When the Master said, "In
my Father's house are many mansions . . . .",[10] he
was talking about Soul. The Soul has many dimen-
sions; it is so deep and broad and so full of beauty,
the beauty of holiness, spiritual wholeness, that it
is the repository of every form of grace.

An individual who has not found the Soul
center is a personality. The word *persona* means
mask: personality masks the true Self. Personality
is fashioned by our experiences in this world. It is
changeable and unstable and does not recognize
the spiritual dimension that is always present. But
the individual who removes the mask by finding
the Soul center in meditation discovers his infinite
individuality, the real Self.

In the presence of the one we love, there is an
act of love that is automatic, and this is giving our

full attention to our beloved. When we live in the purity of Soul, our attitude in meditation and prayer is one of attention, because within us is the beloved Self, the child of God. Loving our Beloved, our God-being, with all our heart, mind, and soul, we pay attention and are obedient to the guidance that is within us. Our love makes us willing to be led of the Spirit. Even if momentarily we forget our relationship of Oneness and slip back into a sense of separation from our Beloved, thereby becoming anxious or worried, believing we must struggle on our own, we quickly forgive ourselves. We return to that inner kingdom and let Soul operate.

Our prayer is:

Thank you, Father, that I do not have to take thought. It is Your capacities and talents that perform and fulfill my soul. My life is an activity of Soul, an activity of Consciousness, and I release it to You. This is Your world, Your kingdom, and I release it all back to Your government and watch You work.

Attention is a vital activity of enlightened consciousness in which there is no judgment, only Love. Eventually, we get to a place in which our inner ear is always open to the still small voice. This is constant prayer, to "pray without ceasing."[11] Regardless of what is said or done on the outer, this inner ear is always attuned, with the attitude of: "Speak, Lord, I am listening for Thy voice."

In living between two worlds, we must also give attention to those who are drawn to us. This activity of Love is the linkage between those who are in this world and those of My kingdom. When we have one iota of truth in our consciousness, someone is going to come along, demanding from us what we have "in our house." On the human level, our highest sense of blessing our family and friends is giving human advice, money, or some form of good. But with the development of our spiritual sense, we realize that we cannot give them anything that they do not already have, because, spiritually, they are Self-complete in God. However, we do respond and attend to them at the spiritual level, beholding their true Self. In giving recognition to the Light within them, the law of Love is functioning.

This act of Love is true forgiveness, replacing the false sense of self that we conceive with true perception. Forgiveness is correcting our concept, *giving* Truth *for* the misconception and letting go of our false beliefs. We consciously detach ourselves and those coming to us from the tree of the knowledge of good and evil and consciously reunite each individual branch to the Tree of Life.

Forgiveness without correction is a judgment, what might be called legalistic pardon. This does not release the individual from guilt or condemnation nor does it release us from a judging attitude. It is only through correction of our perception, focusing on Oneness, that the change takes place within ourselves and in the one seeking forgiveness. This loving action is more often performed secretly. Then, in the silence, the Word of God makes the adjustment for all concerned, and harmony is perceived.

Just as there is a movement and a rest in creative meditation, so is there a sense of detachment in attention. As the Light shines in us, dissolving material sense, we become detached from the forms of good as well as evil. We shift our attention from things "tangible" in the world of effect to the inner peace. We begin to value the inner Presence, the Prince of Peace, so that everything else becomes incidental to the experience of My peace. Eventually, we are so detached inwardly that the ripples of discord coming to us on the surface of human consciousness produce no reaction. However, this in no way suggests a blankness of the mind; rather, we are living in a consciousness governed by Spirit. "Thou wilt keep him in perfect peace, whose mind is stayed on thee: because he trusteth in thee."[12]

Now, dwelling in Soul, we are living as a branch on the Tree of Life. God is expressing everything out of His own infinite goodness, and all that is brought forth functions by the law of God. The ✓ realization of this truth changes our prayer from desire to assurance, from asking to thanking God for that which already divinely is.

Realization is demonstration. We always know where we stand in consciousness by the fruitage in our lives. The more abundantly, joyously, and freely we live, showing forth the fruit of the Spirit, such as love, joy, and peace, the more God is glorified.

"For ye shall go out with joy,
    and be led forth with peace:
The mountains and the hills shall break forth
        before you into singing,
And all the trees of the field shall clap their hands.
Instead of the thorn shall come up the fir tree,
    and instead of the brier
    shall come up the myrtle tree:
And it shall be to the Lord for a name,
For an everlasting sign that shall not be cut off."

Isaiah 55:12–13

The Fourth Day . . .

Illumination Through Love

And God said, Let there be lights in the firmament of
the heaven to divide the day from the night; and let
them be for signs, and for seasons, and for days, and
years: and let them be for lights in the firmament of the
heaven to give light upon the earth: and it was so. And
God made two great lights; the greater light to rule the
day, and the lesser light to rule the night: he made the
stars also. And God set them in the firmament of the
heaven to give light upon the earth, and to rule over the
day and over the night, and to divide the light from the
darkness: and God saw that it was good. And the
evening and the morning were the fourth day.

Genesis 1:14–19

The fourth day is the high point in this
hymn of unfolding creation. This is the
keystone experience in our *day,* the key to living in
the Light. In the everpresent Now, there is full
illumination, revealing the rhythm and order of
the universe, including all manifestations of light
and love. As our Soul-faculties are fully opened to
the everpresent light of infinite Being, we, too,
discover our own rhythm and order of fulfillment.

Remember, these verses have nothing to do
with the solar system as such; the sun, moon, and

stars are but symbols for deep mystical meaning.
The ancients of old spoke of the sun symbolically
as the Sun of Righteousness, which made everything grow, producing spiritual fruitage. This
greater light of the sun represents the Messiah, the
Christ, the Spirit of God individualized as the Son.
Just as the warmth and light of the sun makes
everything come to fruition, so the Son of God
opens our consciousness to the omnipresence of
infinite good, and we bear the rich fruit of the Spirit.

We are fully aware of the Light within us on the
fourth day. Our faculties of Soul are responding to
the Son, and we live in the light of *day*. Jesus said, "I
must work the works of him that sent me, while it is
day: the night cometh, when no man can work."[1]
We can only work when our conscious awareness
is governed and illumined by the light of I AM.

From ancient times the moon has been symbolic of the mental realm. Here it signifies the
illumined mind, which rules the night, that is,
human consciousness. The illumined mind is a law
of harmony to all relationships in the world of
effect. The symbolism here is very beautiful. As
the moon reflects the light of the sun, illuminating
the night, so the mind reflecting the truth of Oneness illumines a darkened understanding. Just as
there is only one sun and one moon for earth, so
there is only one Son and only one mind, unconditioned and pure. And just as the moon cannot
create light itself but reflects the light of the sun, so
it is that the mind is not creative but reflects the
light of the Son.

The darkness of ignorance cannot impinge upon those who have the illumined mind, because they are a law unto themselves. We are our own inner light as we turn inwardly and face the Sun of Righteousness, the Son of God within us. Christ Jesus had the illumined mind that reflected truth and love. He revealed, ". . . I am the light of the world: he that followeth me shall not walk in darkness, but shall have the light of life."[2] When we understand that the function of the mind is to reflect the light of the Son, we are a light, because we are keeping our mind stayed on God.

"He made the stars also." Jesus said, ". . . I am the root and the offspring of David, and the bright and morning star."[3] What does this reference to David signify, especially in relationship to a star? The important spiritual point here is that David identified with his divine Self; he stood "in the name of the Lord."[4] This is why he needed no armor or weapons when he went forth to face Goliath. When we stand "in the name of the Lord," we are standing in the light of I AM, which is protection. In the light of I AM, temporal power vanishes, just as darkness disappears where there is light.

The star of David is made up of two triangles. The upper triangle is symbolic of the Trinity–God the Father, God the Son, God the Holy Spirit, Whose divine nature is Omnipresence, Omnipotence, and Omniscience. The lower triangle is symbolic of individual being: soul, mind, and body. When we pray only with words and thoughts and fail to enter the womb of Silence, we do not feel the Spirit nor have the confidence to stand in the name of the Lord. There is a sense of separation, and the two triangles seem to be apart. The Light hasn't entered human consciousness until individual being is reunited in stillness and peace with the Trinity. In the mystical union, mortality is swallowed up in immortality. When, through self-abnegation, we realize our oneness with God, we are standing in the name of the Lord. Then each illumined being is a "star" in the firmament of Heaven.

Living in the Fourth Day

"The sun shall be no more thy light by day; neither for brightness shall the moon give light unto thee; but the Lord shall be unto thee an everlasting light, and thy God thy glory."

Isaiah 60:19

On our fourth day we are in our high noon; we are in the direct light of I AM, and we are living in the realization that I and the Father are one—not shall be, but one, *now*. As we stand in the full glory of I AM THAT I AM, personal sense disappears, just as our shadow disappears when we stand in the noonday sun. Even though we walk the earth looking like normal men and women, our human concept of self is dissolved almost to nothingness, because the Son is revealing the glory of Being.

There is but one Body; it is neither male nor female, although it can appear as either. It is neither young nor old, nor does it occupy time and space. Body, seen with spiritual vision, is the expression of Soul and can only reflect the beauty of Soul. We have never seen the spiritual body of man or woman with human vision; we see only the shadow, the mental image. We have never seen a dog or a cat; we have seen only the shadow, the mental concept. We have never seen the spiritual, indestructible reality of the Son. But as we stand in the Light, the shadow of mortality and its world of concepts disappear, and spiritual illumination reveals the divine form of the Son.

One day as I was looking out of the kitchen window, I saw a neighbor's cat dragging its hind legs. As I viewed this picture, the inner voice of Truth said, "You have never seen a cat." Instantly, I agreed that I had never seen the spiritual idea of a cat, only the human concept. Agreeing with this truth and standing peacefully in the inner silence of I AM, I was able to forget the injured cat. Shortly thereafter, the cat appeared to be completely free and as frisky as ever, and the owner commented on the remarkable recovery of her cat.

God is not an abstraction; God is the reality of our being, and when we see with spiritual vision, we see harmony. I AM THAT I AM reveals God's name and nature, and this is our reality, which is always functioning now. The trinity of Being—God the Father, God the Son, God the Holy Spirit—is

One, and the nature of this Being is Omnipresence, Omniscience, Omnipotence. As we enter the mystical union of silent prayer, we experience this Oneness, and all that the Father has is ours by the grace of God. It is by virtue of God's love for us that He has unfolded in us His only begotten Self, the Messiah or Christ, and we glory in His name.

Prayer is a moment-to-moment realization of: "In him we live, and move, and have our being."[5] The function of this Consciousness is to progressively reveal Its infinite nature as our individual unfoldment. This makes each day a new and thrilling experience. Our prayer is the realization of the oneness of God and His creation, an already perfect creation that is unfolding impartially and universally from an inexhaustible Source, the I AM THAT I AM.

While there is one individual who realizes his Oneness, the Light shines through, the unconditioned mind reflecting the beauty of Being. When our relationship with our inner Self is harmonious and peaceful, we automatically maintain a harmonious relationship with the Self of our neighbor, for there is only one Self. We love our neighbor, not as our neighbor, but as our Self. ". . . if we walk in the light, as he is in the light, we have fellowship one with another. . . ."[6]

All that most of us seek in this world is to be surrounded by love, to have the capacity to experience love and to express love. Looking for a sense of completeness, satisfaction, and love outside ourselves, we are unable to truly love. Not until we are divested of our limited personal concept of self and can touch the spiritual center of our Being in meditation can we experience Love and Its many facets.

Love constitutes our being and gives us our character, expressing Itself as our soul-qualities of forgiveness, lovingkindness, wisdom, and understanding. Love transforms our experience, our body, and our world. In the atmosphere of Love, we feel an unspeakable sense of peace, for to be fulfilled spiritually by Love is complete contentment. Although we usually do not feel this flow of Love in a material way, It does flow out from us, and we feel the freedom that comes with this all-forgiving Love.

We can accelerate our freedom and our fellow man's freedom by secretly and silently recognizing in those who come to our conscious awareness:

I know thee who thou art. Thou art the image of Love. The substance and activity of your being is irresistible Love, which is omnipresent as your eternal nature and character.

As we pray in this way, building an awareness of My kingdom of Love, we become so permeated with the consciousness of Love that we discover: ". . . before they call, I will answer; and while they are yet speaking, I will hear."[7]

Think of the capacities of those who identify with Sonship-consciousness! One selfless individual who has God-realization is a transparency through which Love operates to uphold a ministry that can feed the hungry, heal the sick, comfort those who mourn, and awaken the dormant understanding.

We have only one motive in our prayer of healing: that everyone be awakened to the Son within and find spiritual fulfillment. Our function is to set everyone free to be governed spiritually. As we meditate day and night, releasing the inner peace, this silent, sacred Influence of truth and love enters human consciousness, dissolving any resistance to God's government. We are not trying to change anyone or anything; our function is only to reflect the light of Love. As we live and move and have our being in the Trinity, letting the activity of the Holy Spirit work through us, It will awaken the outer man to his inner Divinity.

At this high point of unfolding creation, the Light has entered the world, just as the great mystic Isaiah revealed:

> "The Spirit of the Lord God is upon me;
>   because the Lord hath anointed me
>   to preach good tidings unto the meek;
> He hath sent me to bind up the brokenhearted,
> To proclaim liberty to the captives,
>   and the opening of the prison
>   to them that are bound . . .
> To comfort all that mourn;
> To appoint unto them that mourn in Zion,
> To give unto them beauty for ashes,
>   the oil of joy for mourning,
>   the garment of praise for the spirit of heaviness;

That they might be called trees of righteousness,
  the planting of the Lord,
  that he might be glorified."

Isaiah 61:1–3

The Fifth Day . . .

Infinite Abundance

And God said, Let the waters bring forth abundantly the moving creature that hath life, and fowl that may fly above the earth in the open firmament of heaven. And God created great whales, and every living creature that moveth, which the waters brought forth abundantly, after their kind, and every winged fowl after his kind: and God saw that it was good. And God blessed them, saying, Be fruitful, and multiply, and fill the waters in the seas, and let fowl multiply in the earth. And the evening and the morning were the fifth day.

Genesis 1:20–23

After the keystone experience of fulfillment on the fourth day is realized in our individual awareness, the discoveries of the first three days are fulfilled in the last three days. The ideas of Soul, as revealed in the third day, are expanded in the fifth day. "Living creatures" are brought forth; abundant expressions of life fill the earth, each containing the seed of its renewal. As the pattern discovered in the third day is "like begets like," so the fulfillment of this in the fifth day is *multiplication* and *abundance*. The renewal and regeneration of life is unlimited, unfolding from an infinite Source . . . and it is good.

Jesus said to his disciples, "Say not ye, There
are yet four months, and then cometh the harvest?
behold, I say unto you, Lift up your eyes, and look
on the fields; for they are white already to harvest."[1] There is no process in creation. Only as we
limit the flow of the Trinity—Life, Truth, and
Love—by believing in the appearance of good and
evil does creation *appear* to change or evolve.
Consciousness unfolds the spiritual ideas of creation individually according to the readiness of
each of us to receive it. But, in reality, creation is
already complete here and now, and Consciousness unfolds as the completed spiritual Idea. God
speaks, and it is done.

When "knowing" is present, that *All* already is,
then realization of the presence of Truth within
bears fruitage after its kind, although we know not
how it will unfold. As we become aware of the
spiritual qualities of Soul, they produce themselves
and multiply. ". . . So is the kingdom of God, as if
a man should cast seed into the ground; and
should sleep, and rise night and day, and the seed
should spring and grow up, he knoweth not how."[2]

Infinite Life, omnipresent Love, progressively
discloses spiritual ideas of abundance and mobility
to us. Instead of stationary forms, such as grass and
trees, on the fifth day we now have ideas that have
great movement, that can swim in the seas or fly in
the open firmament of heaven. The allusion to
creatures that fly above the earth in the open
firmament is often used in Scripture, meaning that

spiritual ideas of Truth and Love fill consciousness with inspiration. "But they that wait upon the Lord shall renew their strength; they shall mount up with wings as eagles; they shall run, and not be weary; and they shall walk, and not faint."[3]

These spiritual impartations give us the ability to soar above the finite sense of difficulties into the rarified atmosphere of Soul. We are no longer earthbound by the finite sense of self; we are living in the eternal Nowness of Being. As inspiration permeates our being, we experience an awareness of the unlimited universe in which we live. Our body is no longer in bondage to a physical sense, because it no longer intrudes into our thought. In meditation, Soul soars fetterless and free. We can close our eyes, forget our body, and be any place we want to be. We are absent from the material sense of body and present with an infinite sense of Being.

When Jesus appeared to his disciples on the shore of the Sea of Tiberias after his resurrection, he instructed them to cast their net on the right side—the spiritual side. Obeying him, the disciples could hardly draw in their net due to the abundance of fish.[4] The spiritually activated Consciousness, filled with truth and love, is an ocean of unlimited supply. In this state of illumined awareness, spiritual ideas are imparting themselves to us and filling our nets, meeting every human need, and we are abundantly satisfied and filled with gratitude.

In all of spiritual living, the norm is abundance
and multiplication, because Spirit is the only
substance, and It can multiply endlessly. Moses
revealed and demonstrated this principle when
manna fell day by day to feed the multitudes. Jesus
revealed this when he multiplied the loaves and
the fishes. He knew that he was not living in a
material universe but in a spiritual one, that Spirit
is the substance of all form. Therefore, he looked
up and blessed the loaves and fishes, and everyone
was abundantly fed.[5]

That which has a spiritual origin is indestructible, and as long as there is a living witness to this
truth, Spirit appears as the forms needed and
keeps appearing, because the nature of Its source
is inexhaustible. Not only does everything have
the seed within itself, thereby unfolding and
disclosing itself from the invisible to the visible,
but since every spiritual idea is good and always
omnipresent in Consciousness, it multiplies itself
abundantly. "Fear not, little flock; for it is your
Father's good pleasure to give you the kingdom."[6]

Living in the Fifth Day

"... I am come that they might have life, and that
they might have it more abundantly."

John 10:10

On the fifth day in our experience, the illumined mind and the receptive soul are receiving

beautiful impartations from the withinness of Being. At this point we must completely withdraw our identification from the concept of body, realizing, as Consciousness unfolds, that we are unlocalized and unlimited. Since *I* in the midst of us is the resurrection and life eternal, and "of the increase of his government and peace, there shall be no end,"[7] we see that there must be a total transformation of body as well as mind.

This is not patching up the old man; it is not putting new wine into old wineskins. This is a completely new experience. As we are detached from all concepts of personality, we realize:

Who Am I ?? I am not this form I see, neither am I thought; these are mine, these are servants of the Son who is ever one with the Father. It is the Father within Who guides, governs, and directs.

We must practice this principle constantly, silently and sacredly. We judge no man after the flesh, even as we judge Jesus no more after the flesh, because Jesus was swallowed up in his divine Sonship. As the fleshly concept lessens in our awareness, a fuller realization of the spiritual idea of Oneness is spiritually discerned and understood. We no longer look at people as bodies but as individual expressions of the one Being.

There is no loss of individuality when we are no longer concerned with mortality, but there is a transformation of the body into its more spiritual form. Just as the baby's body is transformed to the child's body and the child's body to the adult body, so is mortality changed into immortality as we realize the spiritual nature of individual being. Scripture states: "For this corruptible must put on incorruption, and this mortal must put on immortality."[8] As this peaceful inner transformation takes place in our awareness, we experience spiritual wholeness instead of what the world calls "good health."

What we are aware of as the structural sense of the universe is in reality a construction of human consciousness. The structural sense of body, made up of blood, bones, and flesh, is the construction of thought, a mind formation. Concepts of good and evil give matter its sense of weight and density. The more limited and personal the concepts of life that we entertain, the more dense and opaque our mind, then the more encumbered is our body.

The spiritual Body is not structural. It is incorporeal and invisible, and yet it has form, outline, and color. This spiritual idea of Body is omnipresent; it does not function in time or space. The infinite Being is expressing Itself infinitely, eternally, and immortally as our individual experience, an experience that has no beginning and no ending.

When Jesus walked on the water, he was free of the material sense of body. He had awakened from the dream of material sense by identifying as one with the Father, and, therefore, he was free of the belief in good and evil. After a beautiful spiritual experience of inner communion, we, too, feel as if we are walking on air, having lost some of our sense of denseness and heaviness, because our Soul center is filled with truth and love. We have caught an enlightened awareness of another dimension of Life.

When we are no longer grounded by the belief in two powers, we soar above the duality of material sense in an atmosphere of Soul. I remember an experience when a student called me for spiritual healing. As I was looking out the window, my gaze rested on two doves sitting on the electrical wires. The inner Voice said, "They are not grounded." Then I realized that man is not grounded. He is free Soul when identified as God's child, and no form of temporal power can harm him. I was a living witness to the truth of Being, and there was immediate freedom for the caller.

If the Son of God is raised up in us, the body no longer responds to material beliefs. "But if the spirit of him that raised up Jesus from the dead dwell in you, he that raised up Jesus from the dead shall also quicken your mortal bodies by his Spirit that dwelleth in you."[9] Nothing is clearer than that; this is the truth of Being. The Spirit of God is in every one of us, saint or sinner, but for this hidden Glory to be released, It has to be recognized, acknowledged, obeyed, and adored.

You and I must have the patience that can wait and watch and behold Spirit working in us to disclose spiritual creation. "But let patience have her perfect work, that ye may be perfect and entire, wanting nothing."[10] If it is occasionally difficult for us to rest in quietness and confidence, we need to remind ourselves that a problem is often the prod that awakens us from the dream of mortality so that we can draw closer to our God-being.

When problems come to us, let us not judge after appearances. Instead, let us look at the human picture without any apprehension or desire to change or improve it, knowing that this is God's world, regardless of how it appears to us at the moment. Let us recognize that Reality underlies every appearance and that the perfection of Being is always present, even though we cannot see it. Let us learn to trust in the Lord with all our heart and lean not unto our own understanding."[11]

Jesus asked those who came to him for healing, ". . . Wilt thou be made whole?"[12] Do we love God, Spirit, in the midst of us with all our heart, mind, and soul? Do we trust the Spirit within with all our mind, leaning not unto our own understanding? Do we have the heart willing to do this, or are we shutting out the Spirit by being dismayed?

"Fear thou not; for I am with thee:
Be not dismayed; for I am thy God:
I will strengthen thee; yea, I will help thee;
Yea, I will uphold thee with the right hand
   of my righteousness."

Isaiah 41:10

God-consciousness is expressing Itself as the
individual consciousness of peace and love. Infinity is embodied in the consciousness of Love,
which you are and I am. As we recognize and
acknowledge the Source, we find that there is an
infinity of Truth/Love to be released through us.
In this realization, we now understand that supply
is not material but spiritual. It is the peace and
love we release that is the bread cast on the water
that returns to bless us.

The activity of the Presence within our consciousness is supply. When supply appears materially, it is really grace appearing in a way that we
can receive it. The material sense of good is the
way in which the human mind interprets and limits
the infinity of good embodied in our consciousness,
whereas, when the Son acts as the mediator, the
infinite nature of good is revealed to us.

Because supply is spiritual, it cannot be limited:
Soul is its source and infinity its nature. A fruit tree
is an example of the way spiritual supply functions.
The unseen life of the tree is the supply. The
invisible pattern of the tree reflects the spiritual
idea. The visible form is governed by the unseen
pattern of its unique form of life. Governed by
spiritual law, the tree produces fruit after its kind
for self-perpetuation. But the fruit is not the supply: it is the *evidence* of the unseen Life flowing and
fulfilling Itself as this particular kind of tree.

In every meditation in which we hear the "still
small voice" or feel the Presence, we are supplied

from the Source within. Then the outer forms of good appear in our experience as the need arises, enabling us to give, share, and cooperate out of the great resources of Soul. "While we look not at the things which are seen, but at the things which are not seen: for the things which are seen are temporal; but the things which are not seen are eternal."[13]

Supply comes from the Invisible to the visible, from the unseen creative Principle that works by law to a tangible form of fruitage that blesses. A tree does not consume its own fruits; they are gifts of love to all who want them. The tangible form of fruitage is to be shared, not consumed or hoarded by the Love that produces it. Now we understand why it is said, ". . . it is more blessed to give than to receive."[14] As we give that which comes from the Source, we draw on the unseen spiritual abundance within, and we have more to give. "For whosoever hath, to him shall be given, and he shall have more abundance. . . ."[15] This is a lesson of *letting* instead of *getting*. The lesson is, then, that Life is fulfilling Itself as all creation in abundant productivity under the spiritual law of good.

If the Son is operative in us, we have the meat the world knows not of; we have hidden manna, and we can pour. We pour "My peace" and "My joy," the joy that comes with consecration to the spiritual principle of Oneness. The realization that the nature of God is Omnipresence, Omnipotence, and Omniscience enables us to relax effort and accept God's grace.

God does not need a co-partnership; God does not need our help to maintain and sustain creation. Although we co-exist in Oneness with Him, ". . . the Father that dwelleth in me, he doeth the works."[16] We do not have to pray that apples grow on apple trees. We do not have to pray for fish to be in the sea, or birds in the air. To pray effectively, we must know that we have nothing for which to pray, that God's grace is omnipresent and sufficient to meet every human need. Then we, as living witnesses to the activity of Love, rejoice in spiritual creation, loving God supremely and our neighbor as our Self. We can sit down with a deep and marvelous sense of gratitude and let God's peace flow through us into human consciousness. "My peace" awakens the dormant understanding to the Isness and Nowness and Allness of infinite Being.

Our prayer of gratitude is:

Thank you, Beloved, for being completely all. Thy presence is here and everywhere. Thou art all love and light. Thou satisfy the longing of my soul and fill my mind with light. All is in Thee: there is no outside to Thy grace. I am at home in Thee.

"Thy mercy, O Lord, is in the heavens;
    and thy faithfulness reacheth unto the clouds.
Thy righteousness is like the great mountains;
Thy judgments are a great deep:
O Lord, thou preservest man and beast.
How excellent is thy lovingkindness, O God!

Therefore the children of men put their trust
　　under the shadow of thy wings.
They shall be abundantly satisfied
　　with the fatness of thy house;
And thou shalt make them drink
　　of the river of thy pleasures.
For with thee is the fountain of life:
In thy light shall we see light."

Psalm 36:5–9

The Sixth Day . . .

Immortality

And God said, Let the earth bring forth the living creature after his kind, cattle, and creeping thing, and beast of the earth after his kind: and it was so. And God made the beast of the earth after his kind, and cattle after their kind, and every thing that creepeth upon the earth after his kind: and God saw that it was good. And God said, Let us make man in our image, after our likeness: and let them have dominion over the fish of the sea, and over the fowl of the air, and over the cattle, and over all the earth, and over every creeping thing that creepeth upon the earth. So God created man in his own image, in the image of God created he him; male and female created he them. And God blessed them, and God said unto them, Be fruitful, and multiply, and replenish the earth, and subdue it: and have dominion over the fish of the sea, and over the fowl of the air, and over every living thing that moveth upon the earth. And God said, Behold, I have given you every herb bearing seed, which is upon the face of all the earth, and every tree, in the which is the fruit of a tree yielding seed; to you it shall be for meat. And to every beast of the earth, and to every fowl of the air, and to every thing that creepeth upon the earth, wherein there is life, I have given every green herb for meat: and it was so. And God saw every thing that he had made, and, behold, it was very good. And the evening and the morning were the sixth day.

Genesis 1:24–31

God
act as
Himself

The discernment of the second day is expanded in the sixth day when God appears as Man, made in His image and likeness, full of grace and truth. The beasts of the field, the cattle and all creatures are brought into being after their own kind, but man is made in the image and likeness of God, having all the qualities and capacities of God. He is not brought forth with the animals but is immaculately conceived in divine Consciousness as individual being.

". . . Let us make man in our image, after our likeness. . . ." These plural pronouns refer to the divine Principle: God the Father, God the Son, and God the Holy Spirit. This is the triune principle of Being, Whose attributes are life, truth, and love. Principle and Its idea is one. God, Consciousness, appears as conscious being individually expressed. This Consciousness is invisible, infinite, and immortal, embracing all mankind. As this Consciousness unfolds individually, It is the Son of God appearing. I AM manifests as I AM through the Sonship-consciousness, for each of us is the unfolding of the One.

The glory of God is revealed as the character of the male/female of His creating: ". . . in the image of God created he him; male and female created he them." The Infinite Unseen encloses deep within Itself the eternal masculine and the eternal feminine principles. The male and the female are in perfect balance in each manifestation of spiritual creation. Through the perfect union of Spirit and Soul, the

Fatherhood and the Motherhood of God unfold and disclose the Son, the living Word, Who upholds all creation in its perfection and completeness.

In this hymn of creation there is no human conception, only spiritual unfoldment. The spiritual principle of IS and AS is revealed allegorically for those who have eyes to see and ears to hear. Divine Light, or Life, is appearing as individual being. Love is *mani*festing as the activity of love; Truth is *mani*festing as the consciousness of truth. Therefore, in the image and likeness of Life, Truth, and Love, man is not the limited being he appears to be, but is unlimited Being.

God commands His offspring to be fruitful. As Spirit quickens and activates the Soul-faculties, the fruit of the Spirit, ". . . love, joy, peace, patience, kindness, goodness, faithfulness, gentleness, self-control. . . .",[1] is revealed and replenishes the earth. Illumined men and women are on earth to establish God's government and to impart this legacy of grace to every generation. Peace on earth, good will to all mankind is the charge, and Love is the only way.

Subdue means to refine. The spiritualization of consciousness is a refining process. Just as gold is refined in the furnace of fire to remove its impurities, the human experience is our refining process, where the impurity of material sense is separated from the gold of our spiritual nature. Our furnace of fire is the variety of opportunities that enable us to outgrow our human nature. These opportunities may look like problems, but they are being presented to us for growth in grace.

In our oneness with God, we are given dominion over all the creatures brought forth in the waters, in the air, and on the land. Symbolically speaking, God is instructing us to take dominion over our appetites and desires. As we prove our dominion over our thoughts and actions, our divine Being fulfills Itself as the image and likeness of Love. Then we are given individual responsibility to view all earthly life through the lens of Spirit. As we look at every expression of life, we are to realize that, in reality, all creation shows forth God's glory. "For the earnest expectation of the creature waiteth for the manifestation of the sons of God. Because the creature itself also shall be delivered from the bondage of corruption into the glorious liberty of the children of God."[2]

Living in the Sixth Day

"The first man Adam was made a living soul; the last man Adam was made a quickening spirit."
I Corinthians 15:45

Every thing that exists in heaven and earth finds its perfection and fulfillment in that Grand Colossus, the living Trinity, which is revealed to us in meditation on the sixth day. Our Soul doth magnify the Lord, and we see Him "face to face." The culmination of creation is the love of the Father revealed as the love of the Son blessing all creation, animate and inanimate, with the vision: "And God saw every thing that he had made, and, behold, it was very good. . . ."[3]

The Christ, or Messiah, never incarnates, is never born and never dies; that was Jesus' part. The Christ is the Son of God, without "length of days," from everlasting to everlasting. "I am Alpha and Omega, the beginning and the ending . . . which is, and which was, and which is to come."[4]

Our reason for being is to show forth God's glory through our true identity as the image and likeness of God. We have a spiritual character (glory) which was given to us before the world was. This unseen glory is present in us now, enabling us to have conscious dominion over our world, over our thoughts, actions, and emotions. We have found our peace in our divine Sonship within us, and this inner peace and poise is our dominion.

Jesus revealed the spiritual identity of Moses and Elijah to Peter and John on the Mount of Transfiguration, showing that he was in communion with the law and prophetic consciousness. Then he went down into the valley and was asked to heal a lunatic, and, through grace, the man was healed. We, too, have our mountaintop experiences and then descend to the earthly plane, the lunacy of the mental/material sense of things. But now we do not get embroiled in the insanity of this world. We walk through the currents of mortal thought, putting all discord under our feet, with an inner awareness that Life Eternal is living Itself as our experience now. Immanuel, God-with-us, is a "peace, be still" to every claim of temporal power.

We are told that the last enemy to be overcome is death: the belief of death, the love of death, the fear of death, the hatred of death. As we live in the eternal Now, we see death as an obsolete concept to be discarded, for it is only a transition.

When we grew into a child, we did not leave behind a baby's body, and when we grew into a man or woman, we did not leave behind a child's body. Why should we leave behind our adult body, our mature body, when we grow into our next experience? Let us witness translation of the body by letting the Spirit interpret the universe for us. Then like Enoch, who walked with God and was no more, and Elijah, who was caught up into heaven, perhaps we can experience this way of change. When we know that *I* is not the body, *I* is Spirit, revelation takes place. "Verily, verily, I say unto you, He that heareth my word, and believeth on him that sent me, hath everlasting life, and shall not come into condemnation; but is passed from death unto life."[5]

On the Mount of Transfiguration, Christ Jesus was at that level of consciousness whereby he translated. He proved life to be deathless; he proved the immortality of the body. Consequently, he did not have to be crucified or leave a body to be buried. He could have stepped right out of this world as Enoch and Elijah had done previously, but if he had done so, he would have been regarded only as a great prophet, not as the Messiah. The eternal, invisible Christ, or Messiah, was never born and never dies but is in the world to show us the way of eternal life here and now.

For centuries those functioning in the unillumined human mind have tried to reconcile God to the mortal concept of man and universe, but just as the first and second chapters of Genesis can never be reconciled to each other, neither can we reconcile God to the material sense of existence. Material sense has no relationship to the truth, and there is no way in which God can be reconciled to a misconception.

Scripture says, "Draw nigh to God, and he will draw nigh to you. . . ."[6] We must reconcile ourselves to God. When we come to that place where we are mentally free of all duality, all belief in separateness, all belief in powers apart from God and laws apart from God, then we are ready for the spiritual activity of inner communion. We partake of the mystical body of the Trinity: we eat ". . . the bread which cometh down from heaven . . .",[7] and we drink the wine of inspiration. This feeding is an activity of regeneration and illumination, not only for us but for all mankind, since one with God is a majority. In our gentle, sweet surrender, we are fed the Word of God and are ready to feed the world My peace and My joy.

In this altitude of prayer, where we call no man on earth our father, the activity of the Holy Spirit takes us up into the fourth dimension of Consciousness in which we are taught of God, not necessarily in words or thoughts, but through impressions that inform us and thus transform us.

It is the function of the Holy Spirit to regenerate, renew, and reveal this higher kingdom. As we understand who we really are spiritually and acknowledge Oneness, we reconcile ourselves to God. Then we are spiritually maintained and sustained as branches of the Tree of Life. Living in this awakened state of consciousness, we need take no thought for our life, for we are living as the life of the Tree. The mystical awareness of Oneness makes the full reconciliation and is the repairer of the breach.

> "And the Lord shall guide thee continually,
>   and satisfy thy soul in drought,
>   and make fat thy bones:
> And thou shalt be like a watered garden,
>   and like a spring of water,
>   whose waters fail not.
> And they that shall be of thee
>   shall build the old waste places:
> Thou shalt raise up the foundations
>   of many generations;
> And thou shalt be called,
>   The repairer of the breach,
>   The restorer of paths to dwell in."
>   Isaiah 58:11–12

First we reconcile man to God, then we reconcile all other expressions of life to God. Living in

Oneness as a child of God, we reconcile the vegetable, animal, and mineral kingdoms to God by realizing that "the earth is the Lord's, and the fulness thereof."[8] Then we know that there is no poison in the shrubs or plants of God's creating and no violence in animals. "The wolf also shall dwell with the lamb, and the leopard shall lie down with the kid; and the calf and the young lion and the fatling together; and a little child shall lead them."[9] Even the weather cannot reflect the discord of the belief in two powers but reflects only that changeless reality of the harmony of Soul. It can only reflect God's government of weather, in which there is no destructive element.

A spiritual idea can only express the qualities of God, the attributes of God, the activity of God. When we reconcile man to God, and then the animal, vegetable, and mineral kingdoms to God, we have heaven on earth. "And all things are of God, who hath reconciled us to himself by Jesus Christ, and hath given to us the ministry of reconciliation; to wit, that God was in Christ, reconciling the world unto himself, not imputing their trespasses unto them; and hath committed unto us the word of reconciliation."[10]

In the first chapter of Genesis we have God appearing as male and female. The male and female of God's creation is the compound idea of God, being the activity of both wisdom and love. The female aspect is wisdom, and the male aspect is love. Soul is referred to in the Bible as female, and rightly so, for the Soul-realm is the womb of creation that is pregnant with spiritual ideas. It is in the silence of Soul that we are made aware of spiritual ideas and are given the wisdom to know how to bring them into fruition.

Spirit is love, and love is action. To be whole, we need to realize both the wisdom and the love inherent in us. Love without wisdom is often foolish, resulting in unhappiness and lack of fruitage, while wisdom without love can lack compassion and understanding, appearing cold. The perfect balance occurs when wisdom and love are united in the mystical marriage of Soul and Spirit, and we are Self-complete in God. Then the Christ-idea, that perfect expression of God's own Self, reappears on earth to bless the whole world. "For thy Maker is thine husband; the Lord of hosts is his name; and thy Redeemer the Holy One of Israel; The God of the whole earth shall he be called."[11]

When the mystical marriage takes place, Spirit enters human consciousness through the soul of man/woman, and divine Love dissolves the material sense of separation and death. When Jesus demonstrated the atonement through the crucifixion, resurrection, and ascension, he removed the veil between the visible and the Invisible and made the at-one-ment for all mankind forever.

Paul, talking to the Hebrews, said, in effect, "We have a high priest after the order of Melchisedec, without father and without mother."[12] The Son within us is this high priest. This spiritual Being has no human history or human parentage.

This is the generic Man in the sixth day of Creation, that divine Self, Who is the image and likeness of God. This is our inner Self, Who forgives sins, Who verifies the atonement in prayer.

Our function as the high priest is to minister to the world. "For every high priest taken from among men is ordained for men in things pertaining to God, that he may offer both gifts and sacrifices for sins."[13] The sacrifices we make include withdrawing our gaze from the human scene and keeping the high watch, keeping our vision on the Living One. The constant, conscious awareness of God as All-Presence and All-Power is our commitment of love to God and to our fellow man.

> "I will greatly rejoice in the Lord,
> My soul shall be joyful in my God;
> For he hath clothed me
>   with the garments of salvation,
> He hath covered me with the robe of righteousness,
>   as a bridegroom decketh himself
>   with ornaments,
>   and as a bride adorneth herself with her jewels.
> For as the earth bringeth forth her bud,
>   and as the garden causeth the things
>   that are sown in it to spring forth;
> So the Lord God will cause righteousness and
>   praise to spring forth before all the nations."
>   Isaiah 61:10–11

The Seventh Day ...

Resting in My Kingdom

Thus the heavens and the earth were finished, and all
the host of them. And on the seventh day God ended
his work which he had made; and he rested on the
seventh day from all his work which he had made. And
God blessed the seventh day, and sanctified it: because
that in it he had rested from all his work which God
created and made.

Genesis 2:1–3

On the seventh day, God finished His
work. Creation is complete, blessed, and
holy. By grace, Consciousness unfolds individually
the spiritual idea of heaven and earth, and in this
experience is fulfillment and rest. God rests in
action, satisfied in all that He has made.

On the seventh day, which means *fulfillment,* we
abide in our oneness with the Tree of Life, and the
flaming sword, the spiritual Word, uttered or
unexpressed, is our protection. Now we live in a
finished kingdom, not a world evolving toward
perfection. This kingdom appears as the
unfoldment of spiritual consciousness from its

infinite Source. Our understanding of prayer is spiritually based on one power, one presence, one law, one cause, and one activity, and that One, infinite Spirit, or Consciousness. All conflict has ceased, and Love reigns supreme.

Creation, unfolding from this perfect spiritual principle of Oneness, expresses and reveals the beauty of Being, which is fulfilling Itself as your consciousness and mine. Each of us at this level of awareness experiences Life as the unlabored action of Love, not through getting, but by letting Consciousness reveal Itself as creation in ever new forms of light and love. This new experience of beholding Omniaction is restful and peaceful.

Having completed our six days of labor, we now totally agree with the truth of spiritual creation. In our total agreement that God is the only cause, we have laid aside all material causation as power. We stand absolutely divested of reliance on any human concept. Now, we enter that state of consciousness called the Sabbath rest, which is unceasing prayer. In this rest, nothing is concealed; all creation is revealed as it truly is. We are fully awake to the everpresent Divinity within our humanity, and in this Presence we put our trust.

Just as the Prodigal Son came to himself and said, "I will arise and go to my father . . .",[1] so we have awakened to our real Self and have willingly returned to our Father's House. The Father within has robed us with peace and has given us the ring of dominion, which we had in the beginning.

Now, we are aware of our pre-existence with God, as Jesus was, and we understand his prayer of Oneness: "And now, O Father, glorify thou me with thine own self with the glory which I had with thee before the world was."[2] "And the glory which thou gavest me I have given them; that they may be one, even as we are one."[3] In this altitude of prayer, we are ". . . joint-heirs with Christ . . ."[4] to all the heavenly riches.

Living in the Seventh Day

"For, behold, I create new heavens and a new earth: and the former shall not be remembered, nor come into mind."

Isaiah 65:17

In Revelation, John, like Isaiah, had purified vision and saw, ". . . a new heaven and a new earth: for the first heaven and the first earth were passed away. . . ."[5] The first heaven and the first earth, the material concept of heaven and earth as good and evil, has been replaced by an inner awareness of the finished kingdom, the oneness and allness of God's kingdom within us.

As we rest in everpresent Life, each moment of the day is lived in what Paul described as ". . . the glorious liberty of the children of God."[6] Abiding in Love and unencumbered by mortal thought, we walk transparent as selfless being, and each moment of the day is filled with the bliss of Being, whole and free.

This does not mean that we are not doers of the Word; we are the instruments of divine Will. Therefore, we are responsive to the divine Impulse within us to comfort and serve wherever we are needed. We move in quietness and confidence, without outlining or planning. All action is Love-in-action, Joy-in-action, through effortless, tireless Being. We are no longer living a personal life; we are living in the Spirit, and we now understand Paul when he said, ". . . I live; yet not I, but Christ liveth in me. . . ."[7]

It is the divine Consciousness that does healing work. He who is reconciled to this higher Consciousness is severed from the tree of the knowledge of good and evil and, through the six days of unfoldment, is connected to the Tree of Life. Anyone contacting a person living on the Tree of Life may be drawn into this family Tree and partake of the grace and freedom emanating from it. "And he shall be like a tree planted by the rivers of water, that bringeth forth his fruit in his season; his leaf also shall not wither; and whatsoever he doeth shall prosper."[8]

As we ascend beyond the mental level of words and thoughts to the apprehension of spiritual ideas, we witness spiritual creation unfolding. The purified outer man and the inner Man are integrated. The fleshly mind with all its worldly concepts disappears, and we have a new mind, the one mind that is in the great prophets of old and in Christ Jesus. This mind does not have thoughts and impulses of evil, lack, or limitations, or even thoughts of temporal good. It is just what it is intended to be, an avenue of awareness through which God imparts wisdom and love. Prayer is the listening awareness and realization of these impartations.

On our seventh day, living is no longer a human experience but a divine experience, because we are always listening and receptive to the Spirit. "The Spirit itself beareth witness with our spirit, that we are the children of God."[9] Those who walk by the Spirit walk by grace. We witness that, without doing anything, everything is being done for us. We do not experience success or failure, we do not have victories or defeats; we have transcended the belief in two powers. We are bearing witness to the fulness of grace and truth unfolding as our individual experience. We witness the Father working in us and through us, establishing inner peace and good will to all mankind. Our life of prayer reflects the unceasing fervor of a grateful heart and a soul at peace.

The consciousness of divine Love opens the way for God's government to form the perfect concept of government, business, home, relationships, and supply. We do not form concepts humanly, projecting our will, because we know that this would be idolatry and would violate spiritual law. We only need to be robed in My peace in the realization of Omnipresence. Then, in our oneness with God, we are one with all spiritual being and idea, and what God wills for Himself, He wills for us.

The spiritual idea of government is that all men be governed harmoniously from within through spiritual law, a law that gives everyone equal opportunity to bring forth into expression their individual potential. As we hold to the fact that the government is on God's shoulder, then our form of government will reflect this spiritual reality, first individually, then collectively.

We must not be tricked into thinking that any form of human government can ever give us our total freedom. The only government that can give us spiritual freedom is individual Self-government, and that we have now, regardless of what the outer scene is. The realization that I am as God created me, Self-maintained, Self-sustained, Self-contained, is the highest altitude of prayer. Abiding in this truth, sacredly, secretly, and silently, opens us to God's government. We realize that ". . . whatsoever God doeth, it shall be for ever: nothing can be put to it, nor any thing taken from it. . . ."[10]

Spirit is the catalyst. When the Christ-truth enters human consciousness, upheavals will occur where there is tyranny. Those who have no freedom will want to fight for it, just as in our background we fought for our freedom. Violent change, however, will never establish the kind of government that mankind is longing for. The real revolution takes place within ourselves as we are freed from attachment to the tree of the knowledge of good and evil and are living on the Tree of Life, looking inward instead of outward. What will bring peace to earth? Only with the realization that God is omnipresent as individual being is the Christ-peace restored to earth as it is in heaven. We witness our divine Selfhood, the Christ, operating automatically, and we see the great simplicity and profundity of grace and truth.

A wonderful feeling of gratitude comes into our experience, not gratitude for effect, but gratitude that God *is,* and that God is being God all the time. Even when we slumber, God is being God, maintaining and sustaining the universe and all that is therein, including the body and its functions. We are privileged to be beholders of this priceless gift of grace. The consciousness of Love wells up from within us, and our heart overflows with gratitude. No words or thoughts can express the fulness of love that we feel for that which *is.* "Thanks be unto God for his unspeakable gift."[11]

In Moses' time the children of Israel were unable to enter the rest, the Promised Land, because they wanted to hold on to their humanhood. They could not work as God works, resting in action, because they claimed a selfhood apart from God. Mankind still has never entered the rest prepared for children of God, because it is so difficult to surrender the personal sense of ego, a surrender that is necessary to be a child of God. We enter the rest and work as God works only as we let the I go to the Father.

"But now thus saith the Lord that created thee,
   O Jacob, and he that formed thee, O Israel,
Fear not: for I have redeemed thee,
I have called thee by thy name; thou art mine.
When thou passest through the waters,
   I will be with thee;
   and through the rivers,
   they shall not overflow thee:
When thou walkest through the fire,
   thou shalt not be burned;
   neither shall the flame kindle upon thee.
For I am the Lord thy God,
   the Holy One of Israel, thy Saviour."

                                    Isaiah 43:1–3

God is omniactive. When we sit down to pray or to meditate, we are not turning God on; we are not inaugurating God-action. We have put up our sword, our mental sword as well as our physical sword, and we are entering into the Sabbath rest in which we invite this divine Presence to regenerate and renew us, and to reveal our original perfection.

Our meditations now are deep and pure. We can turn within day or night and instantly feel My peace and My joy. We return often to the inner kingdom and rest in the silence of Soul. We now completely identify with spiritual creation and with our Self as made in the image and likeness of Love. "There remaineth therefore a rest to the people of God."[12]

How far we have come from the anthropomorphic concept of God and those begging and beseeching prayers! As spiritual truths unfold through

our seven days of creation, revealing the nature of
God and the nature of individual Being, our
prayers reflect this growth in grace. Once we know
the spiritual principle of Oneness, as revealed in
Genesis 1, we have discovered the secret of perfect
prayer. As we function from this new and higher
view of creation, prayer becomes a realization of
the perfection of God and His creation as One.

In the spiritual sense, perfection means our
ultimate fulfillment as the branch connected to the
Tree of Life. When the Master said, "Be ye therefore perfect, even as your Father which is in heaven
is perfect,"[13] he meant that we must realize our
completeness and fulfillment as God created us and
then *let* this perfection unfold from the infinite
Unseen. Jesus fulfilled God's plan as the Word
made flesh, bringing the Son of God to the light of
day. "Henceforth, I call you not servants; for the
servant knoweth not what his lord doeth: but I have
called you friends; for all things that I have heard of
my Father I have made known unto you."[14]

The true mystic lives a very private life alone
with his or her own Being, resting in spiritual
awareness, walking the narrow way, which allows
no room for the personal sense of I. The song of
Soul continually sings in the heart of the mystic: "I
am in the Father, and the Father is in me. I will
never leave me nor forsake me. I will be with me
until the end of all illusions, all misconceptions."

We do not stand weary and waiting for our
prayers to be answered, but we rest in spiritual

stillness, uniting in the mystical body of Christ, which is the Tree of Life. The realization of our oneness with God goes forth to all mankind as a healing atmosphere and an enlightening influence without words and thoughts. Then we behold divine Consciousness dissolving the illusions of sense and awakening those who are being drawn to this high calling. Our prayer of fulfillment is:

"Holy, holy, holy, the Lord God Almighty reigneth, omnipresent, omniscient, omnipotent." It is finished, and we are free—free to enter the rest and to joyfully behold Consciousness unfolding infinitely and eternally as completed creation.

"O Lord, our Lord, how excellent is thy name
    in all the earth!
Who hast set thy glory above the heavens. . . .
When I consider thy heavens,
    the work of thy fingers,
    the moon and the stars,
    which thou hast ordained;
What is man, that thou art mindful of him?
And the son of man, that thou visitest him?
For thou hast made him a little lower
    than the angels,
    and hast crowned him with glory and honour.
Thou madest him to have dominion
    over the works of thy hands;
Thou hast put all things under his feet:
    all sheep and oxen, yea,
    and the beasts of the field;
    the fowl of the air, and the fish of the sea,

and whatsoever passeth through
the paths of the seas.
O Lord our Lord, how excellent is thy name
in all the earth!"

Psalm 8:1, 3–9

Notes and Scriptural References

Part I
Promise

The Inward Journey
1. Psalm 139:12
2. Psalm 112:4
3. Exodus 23:12
4. Matthew 5:17
5. See Exodus 3:1–5
6. Exodus 3:14
7. See I Kings 19:11–12
8. Mark 8:18

The Allegory of Adam and Eve
1. I Corinthians 13:12
2. Job 10:9
3. The spiritual meaning of names in Genesis 2 and 3 was researched in the *Unity Metaphysical Dictionary, Science and Health: With Key to the Scriptures,* by Mary Baker Eddy, and *Dictionary of All Scriptures and Myths,* by G. A. Gaskell.
4. Revelation 12:9
5. Hebrews 4:12

The Two Trees
1. John 18:36
2. See Chapter 9 in *A Parenthesis in Eternity*[*]
3. John 10:9

---

[*] by Joel Goldsmith

Notes and Scriptural References

Part II
Fulfillment

The First Day ... Awakening

1. Luke 5:4
2. John 1:5
3. Isaiah 9:2
4. Matthew 5:45
5. See *Practicing the Presence**
6. Psalm 118:24
7. See *Living Now**, p. 38
8. Harper & Row, 1959

The Second Day ... Spiritual Discernment

1. Luke 17:21
2. Romans 7:19
3. Galatians 2:20
4. John 4:14
5. Isaiah 65:17
6. Matthew 5:13
7. Mark 8:23–25
8. Mark 10:18
9. See Chapter 6 in *Thunder of Silence**, p. 49
10. Matthew 6:33

The Third Day ... Opening of the Soul Center

1. Exodus 3:14
2. Isaiah 44:6
3. Luke 1:46
4. Isaiah 7:14
5. John 5:30
6. John 14:10
7. See Luke 8:5–15
8. John 9:2
9. See Mark 14:58
10. John 14:2
11. I Thessalonians 5:17
12. Isaiah 26:3

The Fourth Day ... Illumination Through Love

1. John 9:4
2. John 8:12
3. Revelation 22:16
4. See I Samuel, Chapter 17

---

* by Joel Goldsmith

Notes and Scriptural References

The Fourth Day... (Continued)

5. Acts 17:28
6. I John 1:7

7. Isaiah 65:24

The Fifth Day... Infinite Abundance

1. John 4:35
2. Mark 4:26–27
3. Isaiah 40:31
4. See John 21:6
5. See Matthew 14:15–21
6. Luke 12:32
7. Isaiah 9:7
8. I Corinthians 15:53
9. Romans 8:11
10. James 1:4
11. See Proverbs 3:5
12. John 5:6
13. II Corinthians 4:18
14. Acts 20:35
15. Matthew 13:12
16. John 14:10

The Sixth Day... Immortality

1. Galatians 5:22–23 RSV
2. Romans 8:19,21
3. Genesis 1:31
4. Revelation 1:8
5. John 5:24
6. James 4:8
7. John 6:50
8. Psalm 24:1
9. Isaiah 11:6
10. II Corinthians 5:18–19
11. Isaiah 54:5
12. See Hebrews 5:6
13. Hebrews 5:1

The Seventh Day... Resting in My Kingdom

1. Luke 15:18
2. John 17:5
3. John 17:22
4. Romans 8:17
5. Revelation 21:1
6. Romans 8:21
7. Galatians 2:20
8. Psalm 1:3
9. Romans 8:16
10. Ecclesiastes 3:14
11. II Corinthians 9:15
12. Hebrews 4:9
13. Matthew 5:48
14. John 15:15